NUGGETS

Nuggets
Trilogy Christian Publishers A Wholly Owned Subsidiary of Trinity Broadcasting Network
2442 Michelle Drive Tustin, CA 92780
Copyright © 2023 by Jeremy K. Ponds

Cover design by: Jina Choi

For information about special discounts for bulk purchases, please contact Trilogy Christian Publishing. Trilogy Disclaimer: The views and content expressed in this book are those of the author and may not necessarily reflect the views and doctrine of Trilogy Christian Publishing or the Trinity Broadcasting Network.

Manufactured in the United States of America
10 9 8 7 6 5 4 3 2 1
Library of Congress Cataloging-in-Publication Data is available.
ISBN: 979-8-88738-542-6
E-ISBN: 979-8-88738-544-0

NUGGETS
OPENING THE SCRIPTURES

JEREMY K. PONDS

 TRILOGY

Contents

CHAPTER 1

The Word of God and His Presence

Jesus entered Jericho and was passing through. A man was there by the name of Zacchaeus; he was a chief tax collector and was wealthy. He wanted to see who Jesus was, but because he was short he could not see over the crowd. So he ran ahead and climbed a sycamore-fig tree to see him, since Jesus was coming that way.

LUKE 19:1–4 (NIV)

I imagine that Zacchaeus' friends were wondering what he was doing up in a tree. Zacchaeus being a rich man meant that he had a reputation to keep. He was a part of the in-crowd, high up in society, yet he was climbing a tree as a child would. See, he wasn't concerned about how he looked or what people thought because he wanted to see who Jesus was. You may look foolish to others as you seek God, but if they knew what you knew, they would do it too.

When you are rich and influential, you have access to certain people that the average person doesn't. But in this case, Zacchaeus had to go out of his way just to get a glimpse of this man named Jesus. The question I want to ask is, do you go out of your way to encounter God? Are you desperate enough to go the extra mile to get into God's presence? Or is it only when it is convenient for you? Sadly, most people find it inconvenient to get out of bed on a Sunday to go to church, but they expect God to jump when they are in need.

Amazingly, God will spend as much time as you want with Him and never get tired of you, but people can get tired of God. Tired of how long church service is. Tired of reading the Word, tired of praying.

"When Jesus reached the spot, he looked and said to him, 'Zacchaeus, come down immediately. I must stay at your house today.' So he came down at once and welcomed him gladly" (Luke 19:5–6, NIV).

Out of all the people crowding around Jesus, He chose to come to Zacchaeus' house, and this was not because he was a wealthy and important man. Jesus saw that, out of everybody else, he had more of a desire to be with Him. Zacchaeus desired to be in Jesus' presence, to get to know Him better, and he wanted to draw closer to Him for fellowship.

When you go out of your way to be in God's presence, He will bless you with things you didn't ask for. Zacchaeus didn't ask Jesus to come over, but He came. God notices when you put in the effort to get close to Him, and it will open the door for blessings to come into your house. We know that God is no respecter of persons, but one thing that will separate you from others is your hunger for God.

✦

> So the governors and satraps sought to find some charge against Daniel concerning the kingdom; but they could find no charge or fault, because he was faithful; nor was there any error or fault found in him. […] All the governors of the kingdom, the administrators and satraps, the counselors and advisors, have consulted together to establish a royal statute and to make a firm decree, that whoever petitions any god or man for thirty days, except you, O king, shall be cast into the den of lions.
>
> DANIEL 6:4, 7 (NKJV)

Daniel was one of the three administrators in the kingdom of Babylon. It was the highest position, and he was on his way to being promoted over the other two administrators. Daniel was successful at everything he did because God was with him. His success made the others jealous, so they devised a plan to get rid of Daniel. They talked the king into passing a law that would make it illegal for anyone to pray—knowing that Daniel prayed three times a day.

This is what the devil wants to do to us. The enemy wants to keep us out of the presence of God because he knows that is where we get our strength from. The devil knows that we won't be able to destroy his plans if we aren't praying. He knows we won't be able to carry out God's plan for our life if we aren't spending time with God. So, he throws all these different distractions our way to keep our minds off of God. Let us not allow the enemy to steal our time and make it a point to connect with God more.

✦

"Come to me, all you who are weary and burdened, and I will give you rest" (Matthew 11:28, NIV).

I used to think this scripture was only referring to sinners coming to God. But how many people know that you can be saved and still become weary and heavily burdened? As believers, we need to make sure that we come and spend time in God's presence so that God can lift our burdens. So that God can give us the encouragement, comfort, and strength we need so we aren't constantly being weighed down and exhausted by the troubles and cares of this life.

✦

"So it was, as the multitude pressed about Him to hear the word of God, that He stood by the Lake of Gennesaret" (Luke 5:1, NKJV).

During biblical times, when the Word of God was being preached, people would force themselves through crowds of people to get close enough to hear what was being said. Places of worship would be packed out to the max, and for hours, believers would listen to God's Word and worship Him. The Word of God was held in high regard and viewed as something most precious and very valuable.

Nowadays, people consider many other things to be more important than the things of God. Let us be like those the scriptures talk about who had such a hunger for God and would not let anything keep them from getting into His presence and hearing His precious Word.

✦

"Now a man who was lame from birth was being carried to the temple gate called Beautiful, where he was put every day to beg from those going into the temple courts" (Acts 3:2, NIV).

So, every day he was put outside the temple, but God's presence was inside the temple. Every day he had an opportunity to experience God in a way that he never had before, but he was comfortable outside. Notice that when people don't spend time with God, they tend to rely more on others for help instead of relying on God. God says His people spend so much time outside His presence that it is crippling them spiritually. The definition of being crippled is unable to move or walk properly. Some people don't know how to move in the Spirit or walk with their own God because they aren't familiar with Him.

✦

In those days, the multitude being very great and having nothing to eat, Jesus called His disciples to Him and said to them, "I have compassion on the multitude, because they have now continued

4

with Me three days and have nothing to eat. And if I send them
away hungry to their own houses, they will faint on the way; for
some of them have come from afar."

MARK 8:1–3 (NKJV)

When people come into God's presence, He doesn't want them to walk away
empty. God wants to fill the void that they have and nourish their soul. That is
why the church you attend should have the presence of God in it. You should
be fed spiritually and leave your church feeling refreshed.

✦

As Jesus and his disciples were on their way, he came to a village
where a woman named Martha opened her home to him. She had
a sister called Mary, who sat at the Lord's feet listening to what
he said. But Martha was distracted by all the preparations that
had to be made. She came to him and asked, "Lord, don't you
care that my sister has left me to do the work by myself? Tell
her to help me!"

"Martha, Martha," the Lord answered, "you are worried
and upset about many things, but few things are needed—or
indeed only one. Mary has chosen what is better, and it will not
be taken away from her."

LUKE 10:38–42 (NIV)

Martha was worried and troubled, and Mary was sitting and listening. Martha
was bothered, and Mary was calm. Martha was burdened, and Mary had no
worries. You cannot effectively serve people and not sit in God's presence. Allow
God to minister to you so you can be able to minister to others.

✦

"And the angel answered and said to him, 'I am Gabriel, who stands in the presence of God, and was sent to speak to you and bring you these glad tidings'"
(Luke 1:19, NKJV).

In order for you to be sent by God, you first have to stand in His presence.

✦

Sometimes the tiredness we feel isn't natural but spiritual. The same way your natural body gets from not getting enough sleep, your spirit also gets tired when you're not spending enough time with God.

✦

I woke up one morning and noticed my son next to me, moving his hand up and down across the bed. His eyes were closed because he was half asleep, so I wondered why he was doing this. Then I realized he was reaching for me, so I moved closer to him. When he could finally touch me, his arm stopped moving, and he went back to sleep. We can become tired and feel uncomfortable to where we will need a touch from God. We need to feel God's presence to relax, be at peace, and get the rest and refreshment that we need. Sometimes when we are restless, we reach out to things that will only temporarily distract us from our feelings but won't bring true comfort to our souls. Rest and peace are available to us through Jesus Christ. All we have to do is reach for it.

"Draw near to God and He will draw near to you" (James 4:8, NKJV).

✦

Then He said, "Go out, and stand on the mountain before the Lord." And behold, the Lord passed by, and a great and strong wind tore into the mountains and broke the rocks in pieces before the Lord, but the Lord was not in the wind; and after the wind an earthquake, but the Lord was not in the earthquake; and after the earthquake a fire, but the Lord was not in the fire; and after the fire a still small voice.

1 KINGS 19:11–12 (NKJV)

When God speaks, it is described as a still, small voice. That is because everything around you becomes still and small compared to what God is saying at that moment. God's voice cannot be ignored, and it grabs your attention.

✦

"Every word of God is pure; He is a shield to those who put their trust in Him" (Proverbs 30:5, NKJV).

A few synonyms for the word "pure" are: "solid," "genuine," and "flawless." The Word of God is solid; you can trust in it and stand on it. The Word of God is genuine; it's all true, no lies. You can believe it. The Word of

God is a perfect blueprint for your life. If you live by the Word, it will not fail you. If you obey the Word of God, it will shield you.

✦

"It is when a person walks at night that they stumble, for they have no light" (John 11:10, NIV).

The Bible talks about the Word of God giving us light so that we can see the path in front of us (Psalm 119:105). When we step outside of the Word, we can stumble. When we're not walking in the light, we're likely to walk in doubt, frustration, and impatience, which are stumbling blocks. Keep your faith shoes on.

✦

"For the word of God is living and powerful, and sharper than any two-edged sword, piercing even to the division of soul and spirit, and of joints and marrow, and is a discerner of the thoughts and intents of the heart" (Hebrews 4:12, NKJV).

The Word of God is a spiritual weapon against spiritual enemies.

✦

"And Ezra opened the book in the sight of all the people, for he was standing above all the people; and when he opened it, all the people stood up" (Nehemiah 8:5, NKJV).

This is also why you may hear "stand for the reading of the Word" in church. Also, in Luke 4, Jesus stood to read the Word.

✦

"But He answered and said, 'It is written, 'Man shall not live by bread alone, but by every word that proceeds from the mouth of God'''" (Matthew 4:4, NKJV).

The Word of God is the spiritual food that nourishes the soul.

✦

"Then God said, 'Let the waters under the heavens be gathered together into one place, and let the dry land appear'; and it was so. And God called the dry land Earth, and the gathering together of the waters He called Seas. And God saw that it was good" (Genesis 1:9–10, NKJV).

The Word of God created the ground that we live on, and this shows us that the Word is designed to be our foundation. Whenever you set out to create something, you should pray and speak the Word of God over it first and then begin to build from there.

✦

"So then faith comes by hearing, and hearing by the word of God" (Romans 10:17, NKJV).

The Word of God increases your faith. The Word of God reveals who God is, and the more you learn about God, the more you put your trust in Him.

✦

"Study to shew thyself approved unto God, a workman that needeth not to be ashamed, rightly dividing the word of truth" (2 Timothy 2:15, KJV).

Studying the Word of God prepares you for what God has called you to do. God won't send you out to perform work for his kingdom if you have no word in you. God won't send you out if you aren't familiar with who He is. In studying scripture, the Holy Spirit teaches you how to break down scripture and use it to clear up confusion and bring clarity. How to see who God is and what He is saying. Studying puts you in a position to receive wisdom and revelation from God.

✦

"Husbands, love your wives, just as Christ loved the church and gave himself for her to make her holy, cleansing her by the washing with water through the word" (Ephesians 5:25–26, NIV).

The Word of God washes the believer spiritually.

✦

"For it was so, when Solomon was old, that his wives turned his heart after other gods; and his heart was not loyal to the Lord his God, as was the heart of his father David" (1 Kings 11:4, NKJV).

Solomon is known to be the wisest man that ever lived. When he became king, he asked God to give him an understanding heart to lead God's people (1 Kings 3:9). God gave him wisdom and told him there wasn't and will never be anyone wiser than him (1 Kings 3:12).

Solomon knew that God had commanded Israel not to marry foreign women. The reason being is that they could be drawn away from God to the false idols that their wives worshipped, which is what happened to Solomon. He was given supernatural wisdom from the God of Israel, yet he worshiped false gods in the end. This shows us that you can be wise and still make foolish decisions. It's one thing to have wisdom and another thing to walk in wisdom. The Word of God gives us the wisdom we need to serve God, but when we make decisions based on our emotions that go against God's Word, we can be led down the wrong path.

✦

"And do not be conformed to this world, but be transformed by the renewing of your mind, that you may prove what is that good and acceptable and perfect will of God" (Romans 12:2, NKJV).

The Word of God renews your mind and gives you a better understanding of God's will.

✦

"But be doers of the word, and not hearers only, deceiving yourselves" (James 1:22, NKJV).

It's foolish to hear the Word of God and not apply it to your life. Being a hearer of the Word and not a doer doesn't benefit you.

✦

"You shall not add to the word which I command you, nor take from it, that you may keep the commandments of the Lord your God which I command you" (Deuteronomy 4:2, NKJV).

You don't alter the Word of God to fit your lifestyle. You alter your lifestyle to fit the Word of God.

✦

"Therefore whoever hears these sayings of Mine, and does them, I will liken to him to a wise man who built his house on the rock" (Matthew 7:24, NKJV).

The Word of God gives you a foundation for your life to be built on.

✦

"Jesus answered, 'It is written: 'Man shall not live on bread alone, but on every word that comes from the mouth of God'"" (Matthew 4:4, NIV).

What do we spend more time consuming daily? Is it God's Word or entertainment?

✦

"Like cold water to a weary soul is good news from a distant land" (Proverbs 25:25, NIV).

God's word is good news that refreshes the soul of the weary.

✦

"Anxiety in the heart of man causes depression, But a good word makes it glad" (Proverbs 12:25, NKJV).

The Word of God is powerful, and it holds the cure for anxiety and depression.

CHAPTER 2

Powerful Prayers

Sometimes God won't move in a situation because we're not speaking faith over it. God responds to our faith in His Word. Speaking words of doubt and frustration won't get God to move on your behalf.

✦

"And He spoke a parable to them: 'Can the blind lead the blind? Will they not both fall into the ditch?'" (Luke 6:39, NKJV).

Sadly, many take advice from people that have no direction for their own life. Why allow someone to lead you when they don't even know where they are going? Pray and seek God first for His point of view and opinion and follow His lead.

✦

"Now it came to pass in those days that He went out to the mountain to pray, and continued all night in prayer to God" (Luke 6:12, NKJV).

In this scripture, Jesus goes to a mountain to pray. Mountains are high, so He had to go up to go to it. This shows us that prayer puts you above your natural surroundings and circumstances, and prayer elevates you and causes you to become an overcomer.

✦

"For everyone who asks receives, and he who seeks finds, and to him who knocks it will be opened" (Luke 11:10, NKJV).

In the natural, when you knock on a door, it takes some time for the person inside to come and open it. This scripture doesn't tell us how long we have to knock (pray), and it doesn't say when the door will be opened (prayer answered).

We cannot allow time to discourage us and cause us to think that our prayers aren't being heard and won't be answered. Have faith to believe that God will answer your prayer and thank Him in advance for it.

✦

Then it happened, as He was coming near Jericho, that a certain blind man sat by the road begging. And hearing a multitude passing by, he asked what it meant. So they told him that Jesus of Nazareth was passing by. And he cried out saying, "Jesus, Son of David, have mercy on me!" [...] So Jesus stood still and commanded him to be brought to Him. And when he had come near, He asked him, saying, "What do you want Me to do for you?"
> He said, "Lord, that I may receive my sight."
> Then Jesus said to him, "Receive your sight; your faith has made you well."

LUKE 18:35–38, 40–42 (NKJV)

It's amazing to know that when we call out to God, we get His undivided attention. As many people as there are in the world and as much work that God performs daily, He still has time for anyone who reaches out to Him.

I like the part where it says that Jesus "commanded him to be brought to Him." We can put so much emphasis on us making the right decisions and taking the right steps to get what God has for us. We forget God is the one who will usher us into His promise, into His goodness, to the desires of our hearts.

Jesus asked the man, "What do you want Me to do for you?" It takes faith even to ask God for something. James 4:2 (NIV) says, "You do not have because you do not ask." If God asked, "What do you want Me to do for you?" what would you say?

✦

"Giving thanks to the Father who has qualified us to be partakers of the inheritance of the saints in the light" (Colossians 1:12, NKJV).

A lot of times, when we pray to God, it's about our problems. We pray about what we don't like and what we want God to give us and change. As people, we can be more vocal about what's bothering us or what we're frustrated with. Rather than what we are thankful for.

All through the Bible, it mentions giving thanks to God. Your life may not be exactly how you want it to be, but you can still find some things to be thankful for. Remember that murmuring and complaining kept most of the Israelites from entering the Promised Land. That shows us that you can go to more places in life by being thankful to God.

Think of some things in your life to give God praise for, and you might find that you have more to be thankful for than you have to complain of.

✦

"Now in those days the advice Ahithophel gave was like that of one who inquires of God. That was how both David and Absalom regarded all of Ahithophel's advice" (2 Samuel 16:23, NIV).

David had a friend named Ahithophel who would often give Absalom bad advice, and Absalom would listen and follow his instructions as if they were coming from God Himself. We may ask those around us for their thoughts and opinions on certain things in our life, but at the end of the day, we have to make our decisions based on what God is saying, not man. Only the voice of God can lead you to what He has for you.

✦

"Your ears shall hear a word behind you, saying, 'This is the way, walk in it,' Whenever you turn to the right hand Or whenever you turn to the left" (Isaiah 30:21, NKJV).

In a day, there are so many decisions that can be made. So many different directions one can take. We need to constantly communicate with God, asking for His will in every area of our life. When you are unsure about something in your life, your first thought should be, "God, what do you have to say about this?"

✦

"The effective, fervent prayer of a righteous man avails much" (James 5:16, NKJV).

Prayer is a major help in the life of a believer. We should use it more because it benefits us tremendously.

✦

"In my distress I called upon the Lord, And cried out to my God; He heard my voice from His temple, And my cry entered His ears" (2 Samuel 22:7, NKJV).

Around 3 a.m., I'm changing my son's diaper, and I'm about to feed him as he's hollering at the top of his lungs. "Chill out, dude. I'm going to feed you," I said as I wondered why he was acting so hysterical. We just went through this when he woke up a few hours ago when I fed him. He can see I'm right there with him. I know he needs to eat, and I'm going to feed him. He's acting like I'm unaware of what's going on or that I'm going to neglect him. As I'm thinking about this, God showed me that that's how we, his children, act towards Him.

We know God is our provider. We know our help comes from Him. We know He will never leave us nor forsake us, and yet sometimes we get distressed, depressed, and discouraged as if we have no hope and as if God doesn't know what's going on with us. All the while, God is like, "Don't they know by now that I will take care of them?"

We don't always know when God will handle the things in our life that have caused frustration and worry, but we have to know that God can, and he will come through for us.

We will never regret putting our lives in God's hands, no matter what the situation is. "No one who hopes in you will ever be put to shame" (Psalm 25:3, NIV).

"Then Jesus told his disciples a parable to show them that they should always pray and not give up" (Luke 18:1, NIV).

- Jesus prayed for His disciples.
- Jesus prayed for children
- Jesus prayed before raising Lazarus from the dead.
- Jesus prayed before feeding over 5,000 people with two fish and five loaves of bread.
- Jesus would get up early in the morning to pray.
- Jesus prayed for people's healing.
- Jesus prayed and cast out demons.
- Jesus prayed that Peter's faith would not fail him.

Jesus lived a life as an example of how we should live, and if Jesus, the Son of God, prayed, how much more should we pray. Some things aren't going to occur in our lives or on the earth if we don't pray. Prayer is an act of faith, and our faith in God brings change.

"Then Jesus said, 'Father, forgive them, for they do not know what they do.' And they divided His garments and cast lots" (Luke 23:34, NKJV).

Jesus is in a horrible condition hanging from a cross. He is in terrible pain, and yet he is praying for the people. So, at the very least, if we are tired, stressed out, and dealing with problems, we can still pray for people. God still wants us to intercede on behalf of people who don't know Him despite what we may be going through. He wants us to come against the enemy's plans for people's lives through the power of prayer.

✦

"And when they had prayed, the place where they were assembled together was shaken; and they were all filled with the Holy Spirit, and they spoke the word of God with boldness" (Acts 4:31, NKJV).

One definition for the word "shake" is "to cause a change in mood or attitude," and prayer can change the atmosphere's mood.

That is why it is important to pray over your home and allow the presence of God to come in and bring His peace, joy, and comfort. Especially if you just moved in.

✦

"As He prayed, the appearance of His face was altered, and His robe became white and glistening" (Luke 9:29, NKJV).

There is a transformational power in prayer. Prayer will help you reflect the character of God and line you up with His will for your life.

✦

> And when He came near the gate of the city, behold, a dead man was being carried out, the only son of his mother; and she was a widow. And a large crowd from the city was with her. When the Lord saw her, He had compassion on her and said to her, "Do not weep." Then He came and touched the open coffin, and those who carried him stood still. And He said, "Young man, I say to you, arise." So he who was dead sat up and began to speak. And He presented him to his mother.
>
> LUKE 7:12–15 (NKJV)

It wasn't coincidental that Jesus happened to come across this funeral procession. It was in God's plan all along. God is full of compassion for His people and wants to be right there by them when they need Him the most. Know that it's not over until God says it's over, and when the presence of God is in the atmosphere, miraculous things can take place.

Notice that this woman didn't open her mouth and say anything, and yet God heard her. There is such a thing as silent prayers. Like when you've been through so much, you don't even know what to say, but God hears you.

"You know my sitting down and my rising up; You understand my thought afar off. You comprehend my path and my lying down, And are acquainted with all my ways. For there is not a word on my tongue, But behold, O Lord, You know it altogether" (Psalm 139:2–4, NKJV).

Then His mother and brothers came to Him, and could not approach Him because of the crowd. And it was told Him by some, who said, "Your mother and Your brothers are standing outside desiring to see You." But He answered and said to them, "My mother and My brothers are these who hear the word of God and do it."

LUKE 8:19–21 (NKJV)

We see here that Jesus gave no special treatment to nor made no distinction between His earthy mother and a believer. In fact, He said, "If you obey my word, you are my family."

Since this is the case, why do people put Mary on a pedestal and pray to her? Nowhere in scripture does it support doing this, and this is idol worship. Also, Acts 1:14 (NIV) says, "They all joined together constantly in prayer, along with the women and Mary the mother of Jesus, and his brothers." Jesus taught his disciples to pray, and here Mary is praying alongside them, certainly not praying to herself (otherwise they would have corrected her) but praying to God the Father in Jesus' name.

"I pray for them. I do not pray for the world but for those whom You have given Me, for they are Yours" (John 17:9, NKJV).

We know that Jesus makes intercession on our behalf to God, but Jesus doesn't pray for the world. As believers, that's our job.

✦

Now a certain man was sick, Lazarus of Bethany, the town of Mary and her sister Martha. It was that Mary who anointed the Lord with fragrant oil and wiped His feet with her hair, whose brother Lazarus was sick. Therefore the sisters sent to Him, saying, "Lord, behold, he whom You love is sick."

When Jesus heard that, He said, "This sickness is not unto death, but for the glory of God, that the Son of God may be glorified through it."

Now Jesus loved Martha and her sister and Lazarus. So, when He heard that he was sick, He stayed two more days in the place where He was.

JOHN 11:1–6 (NKJV)

Jesus loved Mary, and Martha called on (prayed) Jesus and told Him what was going on. He stayed where He was. When God doesn't come when we want Him to, we can make the mistake of thinking that He's not coming at all. They expected Him to come while Lazarus was sick, but Jesus didn't come until Lazarus was dead for four days.

"Then Jesus said to them plainly, 'Lazarus is dead. And I am glad for your sakes that I was not there, that you may believe. Nevertheless let us go to him.'" (John 11:14–15, NKJV).

They had seen Jesus heal the sick, but they hadn't seen Him raise the dead. We would prefer God deliver us when the situation is difficult, not impossible. The longer it takes for God to come will result in Him being glorified even more, and we will know that it was Him and only Him who did it.

✦

I was driving home from work and was held up by traffic. I could see the traffic light ahead of me change two times while my vehicle was at a standstill. I became impatient and irritated because it took longer than usual for me to get to where I wanted to be. Construction workers were working on the roads and laying down asphalt.

The next day while driving to work, I noticed the benefits of the construction that had taken place. Though at the time, I looked at it as an inconvenience. The roads looked better, and the path wasn't bumpy like before but very smooth. That's when this came to me.

Isaiah 40:4 says that God will make the crooked places straight and the rough places smooth. You may feel like it's taking a long time for God to bring you to that place you desire to be. You may feel like your prayers aren't being heard. You may be frustrated because you have spent too long in a place where you don't want to be.

Know that God is constructing the path that will lead you to that place He has for you. He is smoothing out the path that will lead you to His promise. God is straightening out the path, so don't get sidetracked. He heard your prayers. Don't lose faith while God is making a way to connect you to what He has stored up for you and promised. Don't lose faith while God is making a way to connect you to what He has stored up for you and promised.

CHAPTER 3
Faith over Everything

"And they said to one another, 'Did not our heart burn within us while He talked with us on the road, and while He opened the Scriptures to us?'" (Luke 24:32, NKJV).

This is why the Bible says, "faith comes by hearing, and hearing by the word of God." The Word of God burns the doubt and unbelief out of our hearts.

✦

The children of Israel had faith to believe that God could deliver them out of Egypt (otherwise, they wouldn't have prayed for 400 years asking God to rescue them), but they didn't think that God could provide for them in the wilderness.

"And the children of Israel said to them, 'Oh, that we had died by the hand of the Lord in the land of Egypt, when we sat by the pots of meat and when we ate bread to the full! For you have brought us out into this wilderness to kill this whole assembly with hunger'" (Exodus 16:3, NKJV).

Why is it that we can have faith in one area of our life but have doubt in another? Pray that God increases your confidence in the areas where it may be lacking so that you can trust God in all things.

"Lord, I believe; help my unbelief!" (Mark 9:24, NKJV).

✦

Faith is a choice, not a feeling. Choose faith over frustration and fear.

✦

Now they departed and came back to Moses and Aaron and all the congregation of the children of Israel in the Wilderness of Paran, at Kadesh; they brought back word to them and to all the congregation, and showed them the fruit of the land. Then they told him, and said: "We went to the land where you sent us. It truly flows with milk and honey, and this is its fruit. Nevertheless the people who dwell in the land are strong; the cities are fortified and very large; moreover we saw the descendants of Anak there. The Amalekites dwell in the land of the South; the Hittites, the Jebusites, and the Amorites dwell in the mountains; and the Canaanites dwell by the sea and along the banks of the Jordan."

Then Caleb quieted the people before Moses, and said, "Let us go up at once and take possession, for we are well able to overcome it."

But the men who had gone up with him said, "We are not able to go up against the people, for they are stronger than we." And they gave the children of Israel a bad report of the land which they had spied out, saying, "The land through which we have gone as spies is a land that devours its inhabitants, and all the people whom we saw in it are men of great stature. There we saw the giants (the descendants of Anak came from the giants); and we were like grasshoppers in our own sight, and so we were in their sight."

NUMBERS 13:26–33 (NKJV)

The children of Israel were supposed to walk by faith right into the Promised Land. Based on the word God had given them. Fear of the giants caused them to doubt that they would be able to possess the land. We have to learn how to take possession of what God said is ours and what God is trying to get us to receive.

We see Caleb was the only one that had the faith to look pass the potential problem (giants) and still see God's promise. Not only did Israel doubt God, but they also complained, wishing they had stayed in Egypt. Those that didn't believe they could receive the land God promised didn't receive it.

Then the Lord said: "I have pardoned, according to your word; but truly, as I live, all the earth shall be filled with the glory of the Lord—because all these men who have seen My glory and the signs which I did in Egypt and in the wilderness, and have put Me to the test now these ten times, and have not heeded My voice, they certainly shall not see the land of which I swore to their fathers, nor shall any of those who rejected Me see it. But My servant Caleb, because he has a different spirit in him and has followed Me fully, I will bring into the land where he went, and his descendants shall inherit it."

NUMBERS 14:20–24 (NKJV)

Later on, Caleb did inherit God's Promised Land because of his faith in God. Doubt and complaining won't give you access to what God has for you. It will keep you from it. Your faith will determine where you go in life and what you receive.

✦

"Then He touched their eyes, saying, 'According to your faith let it be to you'" (Matthew 9:29, NKJV).

God will take you as far as your faith will go. Walk by faith, not by feeling.

✦

"A man is not established by wickedness, But the root of the righteous cannot be moved" (Proverbs 12:3, NKJV).

Our faith keeps us rooted. When we choose to stand firm on God's Word, nothing can move us.

✦

People put their trust in many different things, the wrong things. Many people have more faith in the ability of man than they have in the power of God.

"It is better to trust in the Lord Than to put confidence in man. It is better to trust in the Lord Than to put confidence in princes" (Psalm 118:8–9, NKJV).

Whether it's an average person or the president, it's still best you trust your life in the hands of God than in the hands of man. Man can let you down, and we've all experienced this in one way or another. God doesn't have this ability because He is faithful, and He keeps His promises.

✦

"When Jesus heard these things, He marveled at him, and turned around and said to the crowd that followed Him, 'I say to you, I have not found such great faith, not even in Israel!'" (Luke 7:9, NKJV).

Imagine having the kind of faith that even God would be amazed at. Faith without limits. Lord, increase our faith.

✦

And John, calling two of his disciples to him, sent them to Jesus, saying, "Are You the Coming One, or do we look for another?"

When the men had come to Him, they said, "John the
Baptist has sent us to You, saying, 'Are You the Coming One, or
do we look for another?'"

LUKE 7:19–20 (NKJV)

God chose John the Baptist to prepare the way for Jesus Christ. John told
people who Jesus was and that He was coming. John later gets sent to prison
for telling the king that it was not right for him to be with his brother's wife.
Once in prison, John begins to question who Jesus was, which was odd because
He already knew.

We can't allow our circumstances to change the way we view God.
What we go through doesn't change who God is. God's Word is truth and will
remain the truth no matter what the situation is.

✦

Then a herald cried aloud: "To you it is commanded, O peoples,
nations, and languages, that at the time you hear the sound of
the horn, flute, harp, lyre, and psaltery, in symphony with all
kinds of music, you shall fall down and worship the gold image
that King Nebuchadnezzar has set up; and whoever does not fall
down and worship shall be cast immediately into the midst of a
burning fiery furnace."

[…]

Therefore at that time certain Chaldeans came forward and
accused the Jews. They spoke and said to King Nebuchadnezzar,
"O king, live forever!

[…]

There are certain Jews whom you have set over the affairs
of the province of Babylon: Shadrach, Meshach, and Abed-Nego;
these men, O king, have not paid due regard to you. They do not
serve your gods or worship the gold image which you have set up."

DANIEL 3:4–6, 8–9, 12 (NKJV)

Shadrach, Meshach, and Abed-Nego answered and said to the
king, "O Nebuchadnezzar, we have no need to answer you in
this matter. If that is the case, our God whom we serve is able
to deliver us from the burning fiery furnace, and He will deliver

us from your hand, O king. But if not, let it be known to you, O king, that we do not serve your gods, nor will we worship the gold image which you have set up."

DANIEL 3:16–18 (NKJV)

Then these men were bound in their coats, their trousers, their turbans, and their other garments, and were cast into the midst of the burning fiery furnace. Therefore, because the king's command was urgent, and the furnace exceedingly hot, the flame of the fire killed those men who took up Shadrach, Meshach, and Abed-Nego. And these three men, Shadrach, Meshach, and Abed-Nego, fell down bound into the midst of the burning fiery furnace.

DANIEL 3:21–23 (NKJV)

Then King Nebuchadnezzar was astonished; and he rose in haste and spoke, saying to his counselors, "Did we not cast three men bound into the midst of the fire?"

They answered and said to the king, "True, O king."

"Look!" he answered, "I see four men loose, walking in the midst of the fire; and they are not hurt, and the form of the fourth is like the Son of God."

DANIEL 3:24–25 (NKJV)

Shadrach, Meshach, and Abed-Nego were thrown into a furnace because they chose to obey God and not bow to a statue.

"You shall not make for yourself a carved image—any likeness of anything that is in heaven above, or that is in the earth beneath, or that is in the water under the earth; you shall not bow down to them nor serve them. For I, the Lord your God, am a jealous God" (Exodus 20:4–5, NKJV).

Notice these three were the only ones punished for this, but they weren't the only Israelites present. The entire nation had been taken captive to Babylon. That means that the whole nation of Israel bowed to the statue out of fear. Sometimes you will stand alone when you stand for righteousness, even around other believers. They were unharmed in the fire, which means they were just as safe in the furnace as they were outside the furnace because God was with them. There are so many things that we can encounter in a day that can cause us to fear but let us be bold and stand on our faith like Shadrach, Meshach, and Abed-Nego.

✦

> "Most assuredly, I say to you, when you were younger, you girded yourself and walked where you wished; but when you are old, you will stretch out your hands, and another will gird you and carry you where you do not wish." This He spoke, signifying by what death he would glorify God. And when He had spoken this, He said to him, "Follow Me."
>
> JOHN 21:18–19 (NKJV)

Notice how Peter still chooses to follow Jesus even after saying that a time will come when he will be taken captive and killed. Before, Peter denied Jesus out of fear but now, out of boldness, Peter chooses to follow Jesus to his death. Are you willing to follow Jesus no matter what comes your way?

✦

> Jesus said to them, "Fill the waterpots with water." And they filled them up to the brim. And He said to them, "Draw some out now, and take it to the master of the feast." And they took it. When the master of the feast had tasted the water that was made wine, and did not know where it came from (but the servants who had drawn the water knew), the master of the feast called the bridegroom.
>
> JOHN 2:7–9 (NKJV)

God can do miraculous things all by Himself, but He uses His people to do miraculous things. When we partner with God by faith, He can cause us to become workers of miracles.

✦

"Therefore do not worry about tomorrow, for tomorrow will worry about its own things. Sufficient for the day is its own trouble" (Matthew 6:34, NKJV).

Jesus is basically saying, "You haven't even gotten to tomorrow, and yet you are already worrying about it." We worry about things in advance and fail to realize that God can turn it all around for us today.

"So Jesus said to them, 'Because of your unbelief; for assuredly, I say to you, if you have faith as a mustard seed, you will say to this mountain, "Move from here to there," and it will move; and nothing will be impossible for you'" (Matthew 17:20, NKJV).

A mountain is natural. You can see it and touch it. Your faith in God is spiritual. To get something to move in the natural, you have to first command it to move in the spirit, with prayer and faith in God's Word. Worrying doesn't change anything. Your faith in God can change everything.

"But Jesus looked at them and said to them, 'With men this is impossible, but with God all things are possible'" (Matthew 19:26, NKJV).

✦

"By faith they passed through the Red Sea as by dry land, whereas the Egyptians, attempting to do so, were drowned" (Hebrews 11:29, NKJV).

Your faith can cause you to do things that others are unable to do.

✦

"For I say, through the grace given to me, to everyone who is among you, not to think of himself more highly than he ought to think, but to think soberly, as God has dealt to each one a measure of faith" (Romans 12:3, NKJV).

This scripture says God has given every man a measure of faith. God wouldn't give us faith if we didn't have to use it. You may find yourself in a situation where you will have to exercise faith to get out of it.

✦

Now Mary arose in those days and went into the hill country with haste, to a city of Judah, and entered the house of Zacharias and greeted Elizabeth. And it happened, when Elizabeth heard the greeting of Mary, that the babe leaped in her womb; and Elizabeth was filled with the Holy Spirit.

LUKE 1:39–41 (NKJV)

The angel Gabrielle visited Mary and told her about the baby, Jesus, that she would give birth to as a virgin. The angel Gabrielle also visited Elizabeth's husband, Zacharias, to tell him about the baby his wife would give birth to in their old age. When you are expecting God to do something miraculous in your life, it's good to be around believers who know how to believe God for the impossible. You shouldn't share what you are believing God for with people who doubt.

✦

> Now Thomas, called the Twin, one of the twelve, was not with them when Jesus came. The other disciples therefore said to him, "We have seen the Lord."
> So he said to them, "Unless I see in His hands the print of the nails, and put my finger into the print of the nails, and put my hand into His side, I will not believe."

> JOHN 20:24–26 (NKJV)

For Thomas, he had to see and feel Jesus for him to believe. Often, if we don't see God working in our life, or if we don't feel His presence, we will begin to doubt that He'll come. The problem is we aren't supposed to go off our senses but off our faith.

✦

"Every place that the sole of your foot will tread upon I have given you, as I said to Moses" (Joshua 1:3, NKJV).
It takes steps of faith to acquire what God has for you.

✦

When your faith is limited, you put limitations on God. Increasing your faith increases your ability to believe God for the impossible.

> On the same day, when evening had come, He said to them, "Let us cross over to the other side." Now when they had left the multitude, they took Him along in the boat as He was. And other little boats were also with Him. And a great windstorm arose, and the waves beat into the boat, so that it was already filling. But He was in the stern, asleep on a pillow. And they awoke Him and said to Him, "Teacher, do You not care that we are perishing?"

> MARK 4:35–41 (NKJV)

Notice not one of his disciples said, "We listened to you and looked what happened. God, You mean to tell me that my obedience to You led me to this? You said 'go,' and I went, and this is what I get in return."

When we encounter problems, we'll often wonder if we heard God correctly. Did God lead me here, or did I lead myself? Because we don't see the reasoning behind God leading us into a messy situation. Jesus told them to go to the other side, but He never said what they would encounter on the way.

People can lose faith on the way to where God is taking them. People can lose sight of what God said He would do while they're passing through the storm. Don't allow life's storms to steal your vision to the point that you can't even see where God is taking you. Do you have faith to see in the storm? Do you have faith to see past the storm? If God is leading, you know that you will make it out.

The disciples had been around Jesus for years, so they knew His character and knew that He loved them. Once in a storm, they questioned who He was. We have to be careful not to allow the storms we face to cause us to question God's love or change how we view Him.

This scripture mentions the disciples waking Jesus up, but Psalm 121:3 (NIV) says, "he who watches over you will not slumber." God doesn't sleep on us, so we shouldn't sleep on Him. God is aware of our situation even when He doesn't react when we think He should. God is an ever-present help in times of trouble, even when we don't feel like He is there. Keep the faith during the storms of life. Your faith is designed for stormy weather.

The storms that God allows in your life are not meant to destroy you but to make you. It's better to go through something because you are moving in the direction God wants you to instead of going through something because you're walking in disobedience. In Christ, we will overcome the storms, but in sin, anything can happen.

✦

Some time later the brook dried up because there had been no rain in the land. Then the word of the Lord came to him: "Go at once to Zarephath in the region of Sidon and stay there. I have directed a widow there to supply you with food." So he went to Zarephath. When he came to the town gate, a widow was there gathering sticks. He called to her and asked, "Would you bring me a little water in a jar so I may have a drink?" As she was going to get it, he called, "And bring me, please, a piece of bread."

"As surely as the Lord your God lives," she replied, "I don't have any bread—only a handful of flour in a jar and a little olive oil in a jug. I am gathering a few sticks to take home and make a meal for myself and my son, that we may eat it—and die."

1 KINGS 17:7–12 (NIV)

The problem was she focused on what she had and what she could see. She should have been focusing on God and what He has. Psalm 24:1 (NIV) says, "The earth is the Lord's, and everything in it, the world, and all who live in it." Philippians 4:19 (NKJV) says, "And my God shall supply all your need according to His glorious riches in Christ Jesus." The question is will you believe Him for it?

Elijah said to her, "Don't be afraid. Go home and do as you have said. But first make a small loaf of bread for me from what you have and bring it to me, and then make something for yourself and your son. For this is what the Lord, the God of Israel, says: 'The jar of flour will not be used up and the jug of oil will not run dry until the day the Lord sends rain on the land.'"

1 KINGS 17:13–14 (NIV)

Sometimes we have more faith in things falling apart than we do in things coming together and working out for our good. She had made preparations to die, but God had already made preparations for her to live. She had no hope of surviving until God spoke. This is why we need to be in the Word, to be in God's presence so we can get the encouragement that we need, to walk by faith and overcome what we are going through.

"She went away and did as Elijah had told her. So there was food every day for Elijah and for the woman and her family" (1 Kings 17:15, NIV). Notice when we choose to believe God's Word and are obedient to it, not only does it bless us, but it blesses those around us also.

"Some time later the son of the woman who owned the house became ill. He grew worse and worse, and finally stopped breathing. She said to Elijah, 'What do you have against me, man of God? Did you come to remind me of my sin and kill my son?'" (1 Kings 17:17–18, NIV).

She was so quick to forget that God had just supernaturally provided for her and her family. God was the reason she didn't die during the famine. Just because God delivers you out of one storm doesn't mean another one won't come. The next one could require even more faith than the last one. It seems like God constantly has to prove Himself to us. Prove that He is faithful and that we can trust Him. I can honestly say, as a believer, most of the time, I've worried it ended up being for nothing. God has always come through for me and turned bad situations around. In the end, even though it seemed impossible, God brought her son back to life.

> "Give me your son," Elijah replied. He took him from her arms, carried him to the upper room where he was staying, and laid him on his bed. Then he cried out to the Lord, "Lord my God, have you brought tragedy even on this widow I am staying with, by causing her son to die?" Then he stretched himself out on the boy three times and cried out to the Lord, "Lord my God, let this boy's life return to him!"
>
> The Lord heard Elijah's cry, and the boy's life returned to him, and he lived. Elijah picked up the child and carried him down from the room into the house. He gave him to his mother and said, "Look, your son is alive!"
>
> 1 KINGS 17:19–23 (NIV)

◆

"Now they came to Jericho. As He went out of Jericho with His disciples and a great multitude, blind Bartimaeus, the son of Timaeus, sat by the road begging. And when he heard that it was Jesus of Nazareth, he began to cry out and say, 'Jesus, Son of David, have mercy on me!'" (Mark 10:46–47, NKJV)

Obviously, blind Bartimaeus couldn't see Jesus. He had never met Him before, but he had heard about Jesus. He heard about the wonderful things Jesus did and how He loved to help people in need. Bartimaeus heard about the miracles He performed and the power He had. This is why we must talk about the Lord so that people who don't know Him can put their trust in Him.

"Then many warned him to be quiet; but he cried out all the more, 'Son of David, have mercy on me!'" (Mark 10:48, NKJV)

There's no telling how many people Bartimaeus reached out to for help that couldn't do anything for him. These people that were telling him to be quiet couldn't help him, but as soon as he reached out to someone that could, they tried to stop him. Don't let other people stop you from believing God for the impossible. When everything and everyone around you is saying that God won't, it's probably because you're getting closer to your breakthrough. What if Bartimaeus had listened to the people and stopped crying out to Jesus? He would've missed his miracle that was right there.

"So Jesus stood still and commanded him to be called. Then they called the blind man, saying to him, 'Be of good cheer. Rise, He is calling you'" (Mark 10:49, NKJV).

Imagine the number of people that walked on by this man, not paying him any attention because what he was going through didn't matter to them. When he calls out to Jesus, He stops and gives him His full attention. Bartimaeus may not have been important to others, but he was important to Jesus.

> And throwing aside his garment, he rose and came to Jesus.
>
> So Jesus answered and said to him, "What do you want Me to do for you?"
>
> The blind man said to Him, "Rabboni, that I may receive my sight."
>
> Then Jesus said to him, "Go your way; your faith has made you well." And immediately he received his sight and followed Jesus on the road.
>
> MARK 10:50–52 (NKJV)

✦

We know that God is a healer, but nobody wants to be sick. We know that God is a protector, but nobody wants to be in danger. We know that all things are possible with God, but nobody wants to be in an impossible situation. But this is how God is glorified. Trouble sets the stage for God to showcase His power. Don't lose faith during these times. Sit back and watch God be God.

✦

> And Peter answered Him and said, "Lord, if it is You, command me to come to You on the water."
>
> So He said, "Come." And when Peter had come down out of the boat, he walked on the water to go to Jesus. But when he saw that the wind was boisterous, he was afraid; and beginning to sink he cried out, saying, "Lord, save me!"
>
> And immediately Jesus stretched out His hand and caught him, and said to him, "O you of little faith, why did you doubt?"
>
> MATTHEW 14:28–31 (NKJV)

Walking by faith is a spiritual thing, but we often let the natural elements around us hinder our faith and cause us to doubt.

Jesus asked Peter why he doubted, which is a good question. Why do we doubt God when there is nothing He can't do? Don't let your surroundings or current circumstance cause you to question God's ability. God is still God, no matter what's going on around us. His word is forever true. Nothing can change it. "For with God nothing will be impossible" (Luke 1:37, NKJV).

CHAPTER 4

Hard Times

"So it came to pass, when Joseph had come to his brothers, that they stripped Joseph of his tunic, the tunic of many colors that was on him. Then they took him and cast him into a pit. And the pit was empty; there was no water in it" (Genesis 37:23–24, NKJV).

Joseph's father, Jacob, loved him more than his other sons, and he made him a very nice tunic as a symbol of this. If Joseph's brothers were doing wrong, he would tell their father about it. He also had dreams of being elevated above them all, which his father and brothers didn't like one bit.

This pit that Joseph was thrown in had no food or water in it. If he stayed there too long, he could die. Joseph was put in a place that wasn't fit for a person to live in. Sometimes in life, we can be put in a position of desperation, despair, and discouragement, and our prayer will be, "Lord, if you don't do something quick, I won't make it."

As he is in this pit surrounded by darkness, I imagine that he can look up and see some light reflecting off of the sun by day or the moon and stars at night. There's not always hope in what we see in our surroundings, and that is why Colossians 3:2 (NKJV) says, "Set your mind on things above, not on things on the earth." But no matter how deep or dark of a pit you may be in when you call on the Lord, He can bring you out.

"Surely the arm of the Lord is not too short to save, nor his ear too dull to hear" (Isaiah 59:1, NIV).

Joseph eventually gets out of the pit, only to be sold as a slave to a foreign country.

"Now Joseph had been taken down to Egypt. And Potiphar, an officer of Pharaoh, captain of the guard, an Egyptian, bought him from the Ishmaelites who had taken him down there. The Lord was with Joseph, and he was a successful man; and he was in the house of his master the Egyptian" (Genesis 39:1–2, NKJV).

Now he is farther away from home than he was before. Does peace ever seem so far away? Do joy and comfort ever seem so far away? You just want to enjoy life and be happy, but all that seems so far away.

The part where it says, "The Lord was with Joseph, and he was a successful man" is interesting. If you think about it, this doesn't make sense. Joseph is a successful slave. If God was with Joseph, why was he a slave in the first place? As believers, we can sometimes feel that since God is with us, we shouldn't experience hardship and problems.

Then Joseph goes from being a slave to a prisoner because his master's wife falsely accused him of rape. When in fact, she wanted to go to bed with him, and he refused.

> Then she told him this story: "That Hebrew slave you brought us came to me to make sport of me. But as soon as I screamed for help, he left his cloak beside me and ran out of the house."
>
> When his master heard the story his wife told him, saying, "This is how your slave treated me," he burned with anger. Joseph's master took him and put him in prison, the place where the king's prisoners were confined.
>
> But while Joseph was there in the prison, the Lord was with him; he showed him kindness and granted him favor in the eyes of the prison warden. So the warden put Joseph in charge of all those held in the prison, and he was made responsible for all that was done there. The warden paid no attention to anything under Joseph's care, because the Lord was with Joseph and gave him success in whatever he did.
>
> GENESIS 39:17–23 (NIV)

Through the story of Joseph, we learn that no matter how bad things get, God's favor is still at work. The goodness of God can still be seen. No matter how dark it is, God's light can still shine. John 1:5 (NIV) says, "The light shines in the darkness, and the darkness has not overcome it." God was still with Joseph through all his hardship, and it showed.

Joseph eventually gets out of prison and is put in charge of the entire land of Egypt.

> So Pharaoh said to Joseph, "I hereby put you in charge of the whole land of Egypt." Then Pharaoh took his signet ring from his finger and put it on Joseph's finger. He dressed him in robes of fine linen and put a gold chain around his neck. He had him ride in a chariot as his second-in-command, and people shouted before him, "Make way!" Thus he put him in charge of the whole land of Egypt.
>
> GENESIS 41:41–43 (NIV)

In the same land where Joseph suffered the most, he was blessed the most. Genesis 41:52 (NKJV) says, "And the name of the second he called Ephraim: 'For God has caused me to be fruitful in the land of my affliction.'" There are blessings for those who endure affliction and continue to put their trust in God. Don't give up; God will give you the victory.

Romans 8:28 (NKJV) says, "And we know that all things work together for good to those who love God, to those who are called according to His purpose." Here is how Joseph benefited from his trials.

As a slave, Joseph learned how to manage an estate.

"So Joseph found favor in his sight, and served him. Then he made him overseer of his house, and all that he had he put under his authority" (Genesis 39:4, NKJV).

As a prisoner, Joseph learned how to manage a prison.

"And the keeper of the prison committed to Joseph's hand all the prisoners who were in the prison; whatever they did there, it was his doing" (Genesis 39:22, NKJV).

God will use what you have been through in your past to prepare you for your future.

"Peace I leave with you, My peace I give to you; not as the world gives do I give to you. Let not your heart be troubled, neither let it be afraid" (John 14:27, NKJV).

As believers, we have access to the supernatural peace of God through Jesus Christ. That means we have the same opportunity to be at peace as we do to worry. It's just a matter of what you are going to receive and walk-in.

And all the children of Israel complained against Moses and Aaron, and the whole congregation said to them, "If only we had died in the land of Egypt! Or if only we had died in this wilderness! Why has the Lord brought us to this land to fall by the sword, that our wives and children should become victims? Would it not be better for us to return to Egypt?"

NUMBERS 14:2–3 (NKJV)

God didn't deliver the children of Israel from Egypt only to leave them in the desert. He delivered the children of Israel out of Egypt to bring them to the Promised Land. In the same way, God hasn't led you this far in your walk with Him to leave you stranded. If God brings you out, He already has a place designated to get you to. Since God has continued to show Himself faithful, why would He stop now? No matter how things look or how you feel, keep trusting God. Keep believing. Keep walking by faith.

> Now He was teaching in one of the synagogues on the Sabbath. And behold, there was a woman who had a spirit of infirmity eighteen years, and was bent over and could in no way raise herself up. But when Jesus saw her, He called her to Him and said to her, "Woman, you are loosed from your infirmity."

> LUKE 13:10–12 (NKJV)

This woman was in a storm for eighteen years. It would have been easy for her to give up, and this spirit of infirmity handicapped her and changed her life. She could not take care of herself, so she had to rely on others for help.

But year after year, she kept coming to the house of God and still praying, still worshipping. Still giving God the glory despite what she was going through.

We don't know why she had to endure this for eighteen long years before Jesus came and healed her, but imagine if she stopped coming to church and had given up on God, and she would have missed out on her miracle. When we are going through hell-ish situations, the best place for us to be is in the presence of God.

"'The glory of this latter temple shall be greater than the former,' says the Lord of hosts. 'And in this place I will give peace,' says the Lord of hosts" (Haggai 2:9, NKJV).

The latter shall be greater than the former. Don't let what you've been through steal your expectancy. Be enthusiastic and look forward in excitement to your future in Christ.

> And behold, there came a man named Jairus, and he was a ruler of the synagogue. And he fell down at Jesus' feet and begged Him

to come to his house, for he had an only daughter about twelve years of age, and she was dying. But as He went, the multitudes thronged him. […]

While He was still speaking, someone came from the ruler of the synagogue's house, saying to him, "Your daughter is dead. Do not trouble the Teacher."

LUKE 8:41–42, 49 (NKJV)

Just coming to God with your problems is an act of faith, and no matter how bad the situation has gotten, it's never too late to call on the Lord.

"But He put them all outside, took her by the hand and called, saying, 'Little girl, arise.' Then her spirit returned, and she arose immediately. And He commanded that she be given something to eat" (Luke 8:54–55, NKJV).

"Trust in the Lord with all your heart, And lean not on your own understanding; In all your ways acknowledge Him, And He shall direct your paths" (Proverbs 3:5–6, NKJV).

When we lean on our understanding, we take on the weight of what's bothering us. We cannot think our way into God's promise. As believers, our job is simply to believe, and God will take care of the rest.

And when He came near the gate of the city, behold, a dead man was being carried out, the only son of his mother; and she was a widow. And a large crowd from the city was with her. When the Lord saw her, He had compassion on her and said to her, "Do not weep." Then He came and touched the open coffin, and those who carried him stood still. And He said, "Young man, I say to you, arise." So he who was dead sat up and began to speak. And He presented him to his mother.

LUKE 7:12–15 (NKJV)

It wasn't by chance that Jesus just happened to be walking by this funeral procession. It was already in His plan, and when God has a plan for your life, anything is possible. God responds to our cries, moans, and sadness, and He answers those silent prayers and sends unexpected blessings.

Minimize the negative and maximize what's positive in your life. What we focus on affects our mood.

In Matthew 7:24, Jesus compares our life to a house. I want to point out that a home doesn't need to be completely destroyed in order for it to be rebuilt. There may have been times it felt like everything in your life was falling apart. Really, it's God doing renovations to improve the quality of your life.

I remember when I was on my way to church, and I had decided that I wasn't going to give praise to God. The closer I got to the church door, the louder the praise and worship music got, but I had it in my mind that I would go in and sit down because I didn't feel like singing.

That weekend my car broke down, a family member died, and when we got together with family to mourn together, some decided that it would be a good idea to argue with me about not coming around.

I felt so low, frustrated, and heavy that I believed if anyone deserved to not give praise to God, it was me. Then I read Psalm 113:2 (NIV), which says, "Let the name of the Lord be praised, both now and forevermore."

So during the good and the bad, whether we feel like it or don't feel like it, there is always something to give God praise for. In fact, when you feel the worst, you should worship the Lord the most. Praising and worshiping God when you're in a low place and don't feel like doing it is powerful. It will cause a change in how you feel and a shift in what's going on around you when you choose to glorify God despite it.

"Peter sent them all out of the room; then he got down on his knees and prayed. Turning toward the dead woman, he said, 'Tabitha, get up.' She opened her eyes, and seeing Peter she sat up" (Acts 9:40, NIV).

Sometimes for a person to understand that they can come out of their situation, they have to be told they can. You don't have to accept this. God can help you. Come on, get up. The scripture also says that before Tabitha got up, she opened her eyes. Some people cannot see clearly because their lack of hope has altered their vision. Hopelessness has closed their eyes to the possibility of victory. Encourage someone with the word to open their eyes.

✦

"'Before I formed you in the womb I knew you, before you were born I set you apart; I appointed you as a prophet to the nations.' 'Alas, Sovereign Lord,' I said, 'I do not know how to speak; I am too young'" (Jeremiah 1:5–6, NIV).

What we think puts us at a disadvantage God isn't even concerned about. When He designed His purpose for our life, He had His ability in mind, not ours. We can be so quick to count ourselves out and not try. Philippians 4:13 (NKJV) says, "I can do all things through Christ who strengthens me." If we could do all things by ourselves, we wouldn't need God.

When it seems like the odds are stacked up against you, don't fret. God can still use you to do great and marvelous things because of who He is.

"But Jesus looked at them and said to them, 'With men this is impossible, but with God all things are possible'" (Matthew 19:26, NKJV).

✦

"I consider that our present sufferings are not worth comparing with the glory that will be revealed in us" (Romans 8:18, NIV).

The temporary misfortunes and inconveniences that you've experienced are going to seem like nothing once you've arrived at the next destination God has for you. There is a season of refreshing ahead, so continue to push and stand for righteousness.

✦

God didn't call His people to be subject to their circumstances. Don't accept every situation that comes your way. God gave us the authority and power to change our surroundings by operating by faith.

✦

Then King Nebuchadnezzar was astonished; and he rose in haste and spoke, saying to his counselors, "Did we not cast three men bound into the midst of the fire?"

They answered and said to the king, "True, O king."

"Look!" he answered, "I see four men loose, walking in

> the midst of the fire; and they are not hurt, and the form of the fourth is like the Son of God"
>
> DANIEL 3:24–25 (NKJV)

These three men were thrown into a blazing furnace, and a fourth person appeared in the fire with them. Jesus Christ. A lot of times, we feel alone when we are going through life's fiery trials. We have to remember that we have a very powerful ally on our side who is right there with us.

"God is our refuge and strength, A very present help in trouble" (Psalm 46:1, NKJV).

✦

> When He had come down from the mountain, great multitudes followed Him. And behold, a leper came and worshiped Him, saying, "Lord, if You are willing, You can make me clean." Then Jesus put out His hand and touched him, saying, "I am willing; be cleansed." Immediately his leprosy was cleansed.
>
> MATTHEW 8:1–3 (NKJV)

Getting leprosy back then was as devastating as getting diagnosed with cancer or AIDS. Once a person became a leper, there was nothing "they" could do to get rid of it. No doctor, no amount of money could change the horrible condition that they were in.

What sticks out in this verse is when the leper says to Jesus, "if You are willing." Sometimes we get so accustomed to people letting us down and leaving us hanging that we can accidentally view God the same way we view people. Thankfully God is not man.

"God is not a man, that He should lie, Nor a son of man, that He should repent. Has He said, and will He not do? Or has He spoken, and will He not make it good?" (Numbers 23:19, NKJV).

When we find ourselves in a tough spot, we know God can help us out, but sometimes we can have doubts that He will help us out. If you have children and they are in trouble when you hear them crying out to you, as a parent, you will do anything you can to help. How much more will God help His children when we cry out to Him. God is known as the Great "I Am," and today, He is saying, "I am willing."

✦

"Be strong and courageous. Do not be afraid or terrified because of them, for the Lord your God goes with you; he will never leave you nor forsake you" (Deuteronomy 31:6, NIV).

God made it a point to tell us that He would never leave us because He knew there would come times when we would feel like He wasn't there.

"Now a certain woman had a flow of blood for twelve years, and had suffered many things from many physicians. She had spent all that she had and was no better, but rather grew worse" (Mark 5:25–26, NKJV).

This woman struggled with this problem day after day for twelve years. That is a long storm to be in. It also says she "suffered many things from the physicians." The very people she went to for help only ended up hurting her even more. This happens when you continue to reach out to people instead of reaching out to God.

She spent all the money she had, and her situation didn't get better but got worse. This shows that it will cost you when you put your trust in the wrong people. Jesus Christ is the first one we should reach out to for help. Eventually, that is what this woman did, and she was healed.

"For she said, 'If only I may touch His clothes, I shall be made well.' Immediately the fountain of her blood was dried up, and she felt in her body that she was healed of the affliction" (Mark 5:28–29, NKJV).

One touch from God can change a person's life for the better, and they will never be the same.

And when He had come out of the boat, immediately there met Him out of the tombs a man with an unclean spirit, who had his dwelling among the tombs; and no one could bind him, not even with chains, because he had often been bound with shackles and chains. And the chains had been pulled apart by him, and the shackles broken in pieces; neither could anyone tame him. And always, night and day, he was in the mountains and in the tombs, crying out and cutting himself with stones.

MARK 5:2–5 (NKJV)

Jesus set this man free from the demons that caused him to lose his mind.

"Then they came to Jesus, and saw the one who had been demon-possessed and had the legion, sitting and clothed and in his right mind. And they were afraid" (Mark 5:15, NKJV).

This scripture doesn't say how this man lost his mind or how long he had lived in this condition, and it does say that when he had an encounter with God and was touched by His power, he was set free from these demons and was brought back to his right mind.

Sometimes we focus too much on how things went wrong or how long we've been dealing with a particular problem. We should focus on how one move from God will cause everything around us to change for our good.

✦

"Then Jesus lifted up His eyes, and seeing a great multitude coming toward Him, He said to Philip, "Where shall we buy bread, that these may eat?" But this He said to test him, for He Himself knew what He would do" (John 6:5–6, NKJV).

It says that Jesus asked Philip this question to test him. It's only a test to us because we don't know what God knows. It's only a test because we don't see what God has already planned to do. God knows the end from the beginning, and He has prepared a way for us in advance. We pass the test when we operate by faith.

✦

"So Moab was subdued that day under the hand of Israel. And the land had rest for eighty years" (Judges 3:30, NKJV).

Israel had been subject to Moab for eighteen years, but Moab became subject to Israel in one day. It can all change in a day, and you can go from the bottom to the top in a moment when God moves on your behalf.

✦

Sometimes we don't feel like God is in control because we're not in control. If you cannot fix a problem on your own, it's okay. This is what our faith is for. If we could do everything on our own, we wouldn't need God. Being in an impossible situation isn't a problem because it gives God the opportunity to show you what He can do and that He can be trusted.

✦

"If we are faithless, He remains faithful; He cannot deny Himself" (2 Timothy 2:13, NKJV).

It's incredible to know that even when we let God down, He doesn't let us down. Even when we fall short, God remains faithful to us and stays true to His word. Things may not be the way we want them to be, but let us always be grateful for God's love, mercy, and faithfulness.

✦

"I know what it is to be in need, and I know what it is to have plenty. I have learned the secret of being content in any and every situation, whether well fed or hungry, whether living in plenty or in want" (Philippians 4:12, NIV).

The Apostle Paul went through a lot of hardship to fulfill God's purpose for his life:

1. He was whipped five times.
2. He was beaten with rods three times.
3. He was shipwrecked three times.
4. He was stoned.
5. He was bit by a snake.
6. He almost starved.
7. He went without any clothing.
8. He ran from killers and robbers.

Even experiencing all these things, Paul learned the secret to being content, which is to keep your focus on God and be grateful for the good things.

✦

"And Moses said to the people, 'Do not be afraid. Stand still, and see the salvation of the Lord, which He will accomplish for you today. For the Egyptians whom you see today, you shall see again no more forever'" (Exodus 14:13, NKJV).

This seems pretty easy. The Israelites didn't have to do anything but stand. Don't bow, don't run, don't give up, stand. You see what the enemy is trying to do but withstand it, and God will take care of the rest for you.

✦

Therefore everyone who hears these words of mine and puts them into practice is like a wise man who built his house on the rock. The rain came down, the streams rose, and the winds blew and beat against that house; yet it did not fall, because it had its foundation on the rock. But everyone who hears these words of mine and does not put them into practice is like a foolish man who built his house on sand. The rain came down, the streams rose, and the winds blew and beat against that house, and it fell with a great crash.

MATTHEW 7:24–27 (NIV)

Sometimes in life, we can get hit with trouble from every direction. Problems over here; problems over there. This goes wrong; that goes wrong. You're trying to deal with one issue, and another issue pops up. You don't even know where to start, let alone what to do. But when God is at the foundation of your life, He will hold you up.

"Fear not, for I am with you; Be not dismayed, for I am your God. I will strengthen you, Yes, I will help you, I will uphold you with My righteous right hand" (Isaiah 41:10, NKJV).

✦

"You therefore must endure hardship as a good soldier of Jesus Christ" (2 Timothy 2:3, NKJV).

Believers are soldiers in the army of God. Some battles we fight may take a long time, but eventually, we will come out on top. Our obedience to God gives us victory over our circumstances.

✦

"But those who wait on the Lord Shall renew their strength; They shall mount up with wings like eagles, They shall run and not be weary, They shall walk and not faint" (Isaiah 40:31, NKJV).

The eagle is the only bird that will fly above the clouds to avoid the rain. Be like the eagle and rise above the trouble that falls on you; don't fold under it.

✦

We can spend too much time focusing on what's wrong when we should be focusing on God, who reigns over all things. Give your attention to God and not negativity.

✦

"I would have lost heart, unless I had believed That I would see the goodness of the Lord In the land of the living. Wait on the Lord; Be of good courage, And He shall strengthen your heart; Wait, I say, on the Lord!" (Psalm 27:13–14, NKJV).

There's a reason why this verse says God will strengthen you while you wait. It's because waiting on God can wear you out. The storms of life can take a lot out of you and frustrate you. We must hold on to God's word and know that He will come through for us. You will see the goodness of the Lord in the land of the living.

✦

Here are two verses in the Bible that are exactly the same.
"Give us help from trouble: for vain is the help of man" (Psalm 60:11, KJV).
"Give us help from trouble: for vain is the help of man" (Psalm 108:12, KJV).

It's almost like these words are in all caps and bold letters. I believe this is written twice because God wants to highlight that we should never choose the help of man over God. I've seen how even believers will run to the help of man, not even thinking to pray to God for His help. Remember, our help comes from the Lord, no matter what the situation may be.

CHAPTER 5

Success, Favor and Blessings

"The Lord is my shepherd; I shall not want. He makes me to lie down in green pastures; He leads me beside the still waters" (Psalm 23:1–2, NKJV).

Green pastures are a place of prosperity, and it is a place of peace, comfort, and abundance. A place where you are surrounded by what you need and want. So why would God have to make us lie down in green pastures? It is most likely because we don't know how to get there. This is encouraging because we often feel like we will miss out on God's best because we aren't good enough or haven't done enough. But God is like, "I will make you experience all the good I have for you."

Think about this, for example. A baby doesn't know how to crawl into a bed or a crib, but you will pick the baby up and place them there as a parent. You will lay the baby down in a nice, warm, safe place because you want your child to be comfortable. Well, God is the same way. He wants to pick His children up and put them in a blessed place that they couldn't get to on their own, because He loves us. There is more to life than what we've experienced, and God wants to show us more. We haven't experienced everything God has for us.

"But as it is written: 'Eye has not seen, nor ear heard, Nor have entered into the heart of man The things which God has prepared for those who love Him'" (1 Corinthians 2:9, NKJV).

✦

"In everything he did he had great success, because the Lord was with him" (1 Samuel 18:14, NIV).

God's presence in your life can unlock the door to success for you.

✦

Simon Peter, Thomas (also known as Didymus), Nathanael from Cana in Galilee, the sons of Zebedee, and two other disciples were together. "I'm going out to fish," Simon Peter told them, and they said, "We'll go with you." So they went out and got into the boat, but that night they caught nothing.

JOHN 21:2–3 (NIV)

Sometimes we fish for an opportunity in the wrong places. Hearing God gives you an advantage in life, and following His Word brings blessings. Let God lead you so that your endeavors will be a success.

"He said, 'Throw your net on the right side of the boat and you will find some.' When they did, they were unable to haul the net in because of the large number of fish" (John 21:6, NIV).

✦

"For as he thinks in his heart, so is he" (Proverbs 23:7, NKJV).

If you don't see yourself as a boss, you'll never start that business. There are owners, founders, and entrepreneurs working for others because they only see themselves as employees. When, in fact, they are meant to be employers.

✦

"All hard work brings profit, but mere talk leads only to poverty" (Proverbs 14:23, NIV).

Your dreams will remain a dream if you don't put action behind them.

✦

"So David inquired of the Lord, saying, 'Shall I pursue this troop? Shall I over-take them?' And He answered him, 'Pursue, for you shall surely overtake them and without fail recover all'" (1 Samuel 30:8, NKJV).

Pursue—seek to attain or accomplish a goal. Before you put in the time and effort to pursue any endeavor, you should first consult God. If God sent you, He will give you the victory, and if not, it may not turn out as you planned.

✦

"You say, 'I am rich; I have acquired wealth and do not need a thing.' But you do not realize that you are wretched, pitiful, poor, blind and naked" (Revelation 3:17, NIV).

A lot of times, people will determine their value based on how much money they have. A person can have all the money in the world but be poor in God's eyes because they don't have the most valuable thing a man can have. Jesus Christ.

✦

> Now it shall come to pass, if you diligently obey the voice of the Lord your God, to observe carefully all His commandments which I command you today, that the Lord your God will set you high above all nations of the earth. And all these blessings shall come upon you and overtake you, because you obey the voice of the Lord your God.
>
> DEUTERONOMY 28:1–2 (NKJV)

Our obedience to God is what causes us to progress and succeed because He is the one that leads us in the way that we should go and opens the door for us to receive the blessings that He has for us.

✦

"This is a faithful saying, and these things I want you to affirm constantly, that those who have believed in God should be careful to maintain good works. These things are good and profitable to men" (Titus 3:8, NKJV).

When you live a godly lifestyle, not only does it benefit you, but it benefits those around you. Living for God is more profitable to humanity than money.

"For what will it profit a man if he gains the whole world, and loses his own soul?" (Mark 8:36. NKJV).

✦

"You gave them bread from heaven for their hunger, And brought them water out of the rock for their thirst, And told them to go in to possess the land Which You had sworn to give them" (Nehemiah 9:15, NKJV).

We often only think of common ways God can bless us, like a raise or a new job, but God can provide for us in supernatural ways. He can meet our needs in ways we've never thought of and bless us with the very things we believed were impossible for us to have. Let us not box God in with natural and logical thinking. Remember, with Him, all things are possible.

✦

God can give you favor in unfavorable conditions.

✦

"I pray that the eyes of your heart may be enlightened in order that you may know the hope to which he has called you, the riches of his glorious inheritance in his holy people" (Ephesians 1:18, NIV).

We have an earthly inheritance (blessings) from God the Father that was made available to us through Jesus Christ's death, burial, and resurrection.

"He who did not spare His own Son, but delivered Him up for us all, how shall He not with Him also freely give us all things?" (Romans 8:32, NKJV).

✦

One day I left home to go to the store. When I came back, the parking spot I was previously in was still empty. I parked there again, surprised because this rarely happens. Usually, when I'm able to park in front of my apartment building, I expect not to be able to park there again once I leave. The same day, I left once more, came back, and it was still open. I was pretty shocked. Then I heard the Lord say the word "reserve." There are things that God has for you on reserve that no one can take. When you think about it, there's no reason to compete with anybody. What God has for you is for you, and it will be released to you as you follow Christ.

✦

"A good name is to be chosen rather than great riches, Loving favor rather than silver and gold" (Proverbs 22:1, NKJV).

The favor of God can do things for you that money cannot do.

✦

"But love your enemies, do good, and lend, hoping for nothing in return; and your reward will be great, and you will be sons of the Most High. For He is kind to the unthankful and evil" (Luke 6:35, NKJV).

This scripture shows us that the nature of a child of God is to be a blessing to those who can't do anything for them in return. When God sees this, He sends extra blessings your way.

✦

Complacency is a feeling of calm satisfaction with your own abilities or situation that prevents you from trying harder. Complacency is a dream killer, and it can cause you to accept just about anything. Don't accept anything less than what God has for you.

"Now Joseph had a dream, and he told it to his brothers; and they hated him even more" (Genesis 37:5, NKJV).

You can't tell everyone your dreams. If you tell the wrong person what you aspire to do, they could discourage you from doing it. They'll let you know how hard it is, how much money it costs, how you have to know the right people. Some people won't support others' dreams because they have given up on their dreams.

"If the ax is dull, And one does not sharpen the edge, Then he must use more strength; But wisdom brings success" (Ecclesiastes 10:10, NKJV).

The goal is never to put in more effort than necessary to get a job done. More effort is more work; more work is more time. Time is money, especially when having to pay others. Wisdom gets the job done more efficiently with less strain. Sharpen the edge by renewing and refreshing your mind in the word of God. Ask God for wisdom. Surround yourself with skilled people to help get the job done more smoothly.

Adjust means to alter or move in order to achieve the desired result. Adjustments have to be made in order to reach new levels.

"However there need be no accounting made with them of the money delivered into their hand, because they deal faithfully" (2 Kings 22:7, NKJV).

Have integrity in your dealings. Word travels. Build a reputation for being honest in business. A lot of people are apprehensive when it comes to buying a product or service. Simply being a legitimate businessman will cause other business ventures to come your way.

The Lord our God spoke to us in Horeb, saying: "You have dwelt long enough at this mountain. Turn and take your journey, and go to the mountains of the Amorites, to all the neighboring places in the plain, in the mountains and in the lowland, in the South and on the seacoast, to the land of the Canaanites and to Lebanon, as far as the great river, the River Euphrates. See, I have set the land before you; go in and possess the land which the Lord swore to your fathers—to Abraham, Isaac, and Jacob—to give to them and their descendants after them."

DEUTERONOMY 1:6–8 (NKJV)

The mountain that God's people were on for too long represents a familiar, comfortable, and safe place. A place where you feel on top of things. God didn't call His people to play it safe and stay in their comfort zone. You cannot reach what God has for you while you're in your comfort zone. God has called His people to walk by faith into unknown territory and go after the impossible.

✦

Now the Lord said to Samuel, "How long will you mourn for Saul, seeing I have rejected him from reigning over Israel? Fill your horn with oil, and go; I am sending you to Jesse the Bethlehemite. For I have provided Myself a king among his sons."
　　[…]
Thus Jesse made seven of his sons pass before Samuel. And Samuel said to Jesse, "The Lord has not chosen these." And Samuel said to Jesse, "Are all the young men here?" Then he said, "There remains yet the youngest, and there he is, keeping the sheep."
　　And Samuel said to Jesse, "Send and bring him. For we will not sit down till he comes here."

1 SAMUEL 16:1, 10–11 (NKJV)

The question I have about this is, why didn't Jesse bring David with him? He brought his other sons. Could it be because David wasn't thought of or considered when going to this event? David wasn't even brought up until Samuel asked Jesse if he had other sons.
　　What this shows us is that if people don't include or consider you, it's okay. If you get left out because people don't think of you, it's okay. What matters is that God is mindful of you. Psalm 8:4 (NKJV) says, "What is man that you are mindful of him." What will make the difference in your life is you being on God's mind and in His will.

So, David's earthly father and his brothers didn't even make it a point to invite him to the table, to this sacrificial event. He was left out entirely; he didn't even get an invitation. You can imagine while this is going on, David is off in the distance seeing the gathering that is taking place without him. He probably could smell the food that was being prepared. David could hear the laughter and commotion of the people there. Maybe he didn't have the confidence to come over and see what was going on because he was used to being left.

Would you rather be invited by men or chosen by God? When you are chosen by God, walking in your calling, you are set apart anyway. You won't fit in.

David's father, his brothers, and the people of Bethlehem didn't invite David to the party, but they were about to find out that God had already made him the guest of honor. Notice how in this verse, Samuel says, "Send for him; we will not sit down until he arrives." Samuel had more respect for David than his own family did.

Sometimes people familiar with you, who knew you before you became a believer, can't see what God is doing in your life, but a stranger can. A stranger can see your potential and greatness. So, this party wasn't going to start until David walked in.

> So he sent and brought him in. Now he was ruddy, with bright eyes, and good-looking. And the Lord said, "Arise, anoint him; for this is the one!" Then Samuel took the horn of oil and anointed him in the midst of his brothers; and the Spirit of the Lord came upon David from that day forward. So Samuel arose and went to Ramah.
>
> 1 SAMUEL 16:12–13 (NKJV)

It says he anointed him in the midst of his brothers. The very people that looked down on you and counted you out, God will give them a front-row seat to your elevation. A free ticket to your promotion party. "You prepare a table before me in the presence of my enemies; You anoint my head with oil; My cup runs over" (Psalm 23:5, NKJV). And this is how we know David's brothers treated him differently. When Goliath was blaspheming God, and the Israelites were scared to confront him, David asked what would become of the man who defeated him. His brother overheard him asking, this is what happened.

> Now Eliab his oldest brother heard when he spoke to the men; and Eliab's anger was aroused against David, and he said, "Why did you come down here? And with whom have you left those few

sheep in the wilderness? I know your pride and the insolence of your heart, for you have come down to see the battle."

1 SAMUEL 17:28 (NKJV)

What I like about this story is that David hasn't said one word. He's not complaining about having to watch the sheep and being left out. He's just sitting back, putting his work in, and God comes along and promotes him. You don't have to prove yourself to anybody or even respond to the naysayers. God has a position designated just for you that no one can take, and when it's your time, God will elevate you.

✦

"And do not be conformed to this world, but be transformed by the renewing of your mind, that you may prove what is that good and acceptable and perfect will of God" (Romans 12:2, NKJV).

Having the same old mindset will keep you in the same old place. Let God change the way you think.

✦

Now Deborah, a prophetess, the wife of Lapidoth, was judging Israel at that time. And she would sit under the palm tree of Deborah between Ramah and Bethel in the mountains of Ephraim. And the children of Israel came up to her for judgment. Then she sent and called for Barak the son of Abinoam from Kedesh in Naphtali, and said to him, "Has not the Lord God of Israel commanded, 'Go and deploy troops at Mount Tabor; take with you ten thousand men of the sons of Naphtali and of the sons of Zebulun; and against you I will deploy Sisera, the commander of Jabin's army, with his chariots and his multitude at the River Kishon; and I will deliver him into your hand'?"

And Barak said to her, "If you will go with me, then I will go; but if you will not go with me, I will not go!"

JUDGES 4:4–8 (NKJV)

When a man is lacking confidence, sometimes all he needs is a woman by his side. The support of a woman can help a man step out by faith and do what God has called him to do. A woman who knows how to pray and loves the Lord. A woman who God confides in.

"He who finds a wife finds a good thing, And obtains favor from the Lord" (Proverbs 18:22, NKJV).

✦

"Do you see a man who excels in his work? He will stand before kings; He will not stand before unknown men" (Proverbs 22:29, NKJV).

Hard work and success will usher you into the presence of renowned men.

> Then one of them, named Agabus, stood up and showed by the Spirit that there was going to be a great famine throughout all the world, which also happened in the days of Claudius Caesar. Then the disciples, each according to his ability, determined to send relief to the brethren dwelling in Judea.
>
> ACTS 11:28–29 (NKJV)

We could be in an impoverished area while the economy is terrible, and God could still give us the resources we need. The conditions we may be in or the circumstances around us cannot prevent God from being who He is. A provider. There is no lack or debt in God's economy. God has infinite riches, and we are a part of His kingdom, so that means we have access to unlimited aid.

✦

> Then He said: "A certain man had two sons. And the younger of them said to his father, 'Father, give me the portion of goods that falls to me.' So he divided to them his livelihood. And not many days after, the younger son gathered all together, journeyed to a far country, and there wasted his possessions with prodigal living."
>
> LUKE 15:11–13 (NKJV)

Like the young son, many people want freedom without responsibility. Money brings certain liberties. Notice the older son also received his inheritance, but he stayed with his father. Be careful not to allow money to cause you to drift from your relationship with your Father God.

✦

If you tell God you can't, it's almost like you're saying, "Lord, you don't have the ability to do this through me." It's never been about what you can do but what God can do through you.

"But the people who know their God shall be strong, and carry out great exploits" (Daniel 11:32, NKJV).

CHAPTER 6

Opposition

"Then He said to the disciples, 'It is impossible that no offenses should come, but woe to him through whom they do come!'" (Luke 17:1, NKJV).

I believe now more than ever that God wants His people to guard their hearts against offense. Offenses may come but don't let them cause you to harbor bitterness and unforgiveness. Even from a medical standpoint, it shows that our bodies are not meant to hold on to negative emotions, and they, in return, have a negative effect on us.

"Above all else, guard your heart, for everything you do flows from it" (Proverbs 4:23, NIV).

"For a great and effective door has opened to me, and there are many adversaries" (1 Corinthians 16:9, NKJV).

Opposition often accompanies opportunity. The degree of opposition that you face can be a clear indicator of the great breakthrough and elevation that lies ahead. In fact, you wouldn't be attacked if there wasn't greatness on the inside of you. So don't stop; push through the opposition and keep going.

"The discretion of a man makes him slow to anger, And his glory is to overlook a transgression" (Proverbs 19:11, NKJV).

Sometimes the strongest person has to show the most restraint.

Then this Daniel distinguished himself above the governors and satraps, because an excellent spirit was in him; and the king gave thought to setting him over the whole realm. So the governors and satraps sought to find some charge against Daniel concerning the kingdom; but they could find no charge or fault, because he was faithful; nor was there any error or fault found in him.

DANIEL 6:3–4 (NKJV)

You could be doing everything right, yet people can still look for a reason to condemn you. I want to point out how this verse says that David had an excellent spirit in him. But what kind of spirit did the satraps and governors have in them? We have to be aware that sometimes the spirit inside a person will cause them to come against us, simply because of the Holy Spirit that is on the inside of us.

> So the king gave the command, and they brought Daniel and cast him into the den of lions. But the king spoke, saying to Daniel, "Your God, whom you serve continually, He will deliver you." Then a stone was brought and laid on the mouth of the den, and the king sealed it with his own signet ring and with the signets of his lords, that the purpose concerning Daniel might not be changed.
>
> DANIEL 6:16–17 (NKJV)

The king's seal was supposed to seal the fate of Daniel like a conviction and sentence. God ends up sending an angel to shut the mouths of the lions, keeping Daniel safe. The enemy can't seal the fate of a believer. Our lives are in God's hands.

> The Philistines stood on a mountain on one side, and Israel stood on a mountain on the other side, with a valley between them. And a champion went out from the camp of the Philistines, named Goliath, from Gath, whose height was six cubits and a span.
> [...]
> And the Philistine drew near and presented himself forty days, morning and evening.
>
> 1 SAMUEL 17:3–4, 16 (NKJV)

For forty days, the people of Israel looked at and talked about their problem but did nothing about it. Fear causes people to avoid their problems and observe them from afar. Faith moves people to engage, overcome, and conquer the obstacles and issues that are before them. God has called His people to confront and subdue whatever stands in their way. If we do not face our problems, they will not go away.

✦

He went to Nazareth, where he had been brought up, and on the
Sabbath day he went into the synagogue, as was his custom. He
stood up to read […]

All the people in the synagogue were furious when they
heard this. They got up, drove him out of the town, and took him
to the brow of the hill on which the town was built, in order to
throw him off the cliff. But he walked right through the crowd
and went on his way.

LUKE 4:16, 28–30 (NIV)

It's ironic how all the people got upset with Jesus for reading the scripture when
they came into the synagogue to hear the scriptures. Some people only want to
hear about the blessings of God and what God can do for them, and they don't
want to hear about sin, demons, repentance, and obedience.

Also, notice how Jesus waited until He was backed to the edge of a
cliff to walk pass the angry crowd. He waited to be in that position to show us
how you can find yourself in a situation that you can't run from. All you can
do is trust God and walk by faith to come out of it.

✦

"Now these are the nations which the Lord left, that He might test Israel by them,
that is, all who had not known any of the wars in Canaan (this was only so that
the generations of the children of Israel might be taught to know war, at least
those who had not formerly known it)" (Judges 3:1–2, NKJV).

You won't learn how to fight unless there is opposition coming against
you. You won't truly understand how your faith is a weapon until you are being
attacked by fear, doubt, and discouragement. Every soldier of Christ Jesus will
go through battles. The Bible tells us to fight the good fight of faith. To trust
God no matter what's coming against us and keep pushing forward to do what
He created us to do. If we cannot fight for ourselves, how will we know how
to fight for others?

✦

"And He was casting out a demon, and it was mute. So it was, when the demon
had gone out, that the mute spoke; and the multitudes marveled. But some of
them said, 'He casts out demons by Beelzebub, the ruler of the demons'" (Luke
11:14–15, NKJV).

After Jesus helped this man, some people were trying to discredit the good He had just done and make Him look bad. Some people you encounter in life are set on making you look bad no matter what you do. That is why we should never be dependent on other people's acceptance to the point where we become discouraged and uncomfortable if we don't get it. When God is pleased with you, that's all the acceptance you need.

✦

When those around Him saw what was going to happen, they said to Him, "Lord, shall we strike with the sword?" And one of them struck the servant of the high priest and cut off his right ear.
    But Jesus answered and said, "Permit even this." And He touched his ear and healed him.

LUKE 22:49–51 (NKJV)

Peter, a follower of Jesus, cut off a servant's ear, and Jesus had to heal him. Some people come into church for Jesus and get cut (hurt) by someone who is supposed to be a follower of Christ. Someone who is a leader in the church. Someone they considered a friend. Church hurt cuts deep, and God has to heal people from this kind of wound supernaturally.
    Church hurt seems to be a weapon that the devil uses to keep people away from God. Remember, the devil will use anyone to carry out his plans if they let him in and allow him to. If you ask some people why they don't go to church anymore, they often tell you how they were hurt in church. So, God not only gets blamed for what the devil does, but He also takes the blame when people misrepresent Him.
    Let's keep in mind what Jesus spoke to Peter.
    "Again Jesus said, 'Simon son of John, do you love me?' He answered, 'Yes, Lord, you know that I love you.' Jesus said, 'Take care of my sheep'" (John 21:16, NIV).

✦

"Now whatever city or town you enter, inquire who in it is worthy, and stay there till you go out" (Matthew 10:11, NKJV).
    I believe people get mistreated when they are in the presence of people that don't understand their value and cannot see what God has placed in them. Some people aren't worthy of your company.

◆

From that time Jesus began to show to His disciples that He must go to Jerusalem, and suffer many things from the elders and chief priests and scribes, and be killed, and be raised the third day.

Then Peter took Him aside and began to rebuke Him, saying, "Far be it from You, Lord; this shall not happen to You!"

But He turned and said to Peter, "Get behind Me, Satan! You are an offense to Me, for you are not mindful of the things of God, but the things of men."

MATTHEW 16:21–23 (NKJV)

Peter was one of Jesus' disciples, yet he was speaking against God's will for Jesus' life, and he tried to keep Him from going to the cross. This shows that even believers can discourage you from doing what God created you to do, simply because they don't understand it. Most people won't comprehend your destiny. That is why you have to know God's will for your life for yourself and not try to lean on other people for their opinion or approval on it.

◆

"After these things Jesus walked in Galilee; for He did not want to walk in Judea, because the Jews sought to kill Him" (John 7:1, NKJV).

God wasn't going to let anyone take Jesus before His appointed time. Yet Jesus still used wisdom and stayed away from certain areas where there was no purpose for Him to be there.

◆

"Now a certain young man followed Him, having a linen cloth thrown around his naked body. And the young men laid hold of him, and he left the linen cloth and fled from them naked" (Mark 14:51–52, NKJV).

You can always tell what level of spiritual maturity a person is at by how they handle opposition. This young man wasn't spiritually mature. The linen cloth that this young man wore was similar to what people wore to bed, like pajamas. But Ephesians 6:13 (NKJV) says we are to "therefore take up the whole armor of God, that you may be able to withstand in the evil day." Not run in the evil day. This scripture also says that young men tried to bind him and arrest him. They were young, so they weren't fully strong. This was a small attack, a minor opposition. If the young man had faith and diligence, he would have been able to withstand this and continue to follow Christ, but he ran. When you get saved, it's not the end. You are a babe spiritually, so you have to mature and grow up spiritually.

✦

"Yet in all these things we are more than conquerors through Him who loved us" (Romans 8:37, NKJV).

This tells us that there will be some things we encounter in our life that we need to overcome. You cannot be a conqueror unless you first have something to conquer. Another word for conqueror is "winner." We weren't born to lose. God created us to win. The only time in the Bible when Israel was defeated in battle is when they stepped outside of God's will and were disobedient.

If we tell God, "We can't," it's like we're saying, "God, you can't do this through me." We know that the Bible says that we can do all things through Christ who strengthens us (Philippians 4:13). We can endure and overcome. We can conquer whatever comes our way because of our connection to Jesus Christ.

✦

"The Jews then responded to him, 'What sign can you show us to prove your authority to do all this?'" (John 2:18, NIV).

There will always be people who will challenge you to prove yourself. If you feel the need to prove yourself to people, you will continue to do it for the rest of your life because there will always be doubters.

✦

Now there stood by the cross of Jesus His mother, and His mother's sister, Mary the wife of Clopas, and Mary Magdalene. When Jesus therefore saw His mother, and the disciple whom He loved standing by, He said to His mother, "Woman, behold your son!" Then He said to the disciple, "Behold your mother!" And from that hour that disciple took her to his own home.

JOHN 19:25–27 (NKJV)

Jesus knew Mary would be in good hands with John caring for her like his own mother. Out of the twelve disciples, Jesus chose John to be Mary's new son.

This says a lot about John's character. Many people want to do big things for the Lord, but what is their character like? It should reflect Christ's character.

Another reason why Jesus chose John to take care of Mary is because He saw him standing there. In fact, John was the only disciple present at Jesus' crucifixion. See, when you choose to stand by Jesus, stand by the Word of God; He will entrust you with great responsibility.

✦

"But Jesus did not commit Himself to them, because He knew all men, and had no need that anyone should testify of man, for He knew what was in man" (John 2:24–25, NKJV).

Jesus knew the true character of the people He came in contact with. He could see past their outward appearance into their hearts, and because of this, He could not be deceived by man.

So many times, people are being deceived, taken advantage of, and stabbed in the back by people they thought were their friends. People who they believed were loyal and had a love for them. Now more than ever, people need to pray for spiritual discernment, especially when it comes to letting people into their lives. Spiritual discernment will help you identify wolves in sheep's clothing.

✦

From that time on Jesus began to explain to his disciples that he must go to Jerusalem and suffer many things at the hands of the elders, the chief priests and the teachers of the law, and that he must be killed and on the third day be raised to life.

Peter took him aside and began to rebuke him. "Never, Lord!" he said. "This shall never happen to you!"

MATTHEW 16:21–22 (NIV)

Peter was one of the twelve disciples, yet he spoke against God's will for Jesus' life. This shows that even fellow believers can discourage you from doing what God created you to do—opposing God's will for your life. Most people won't understand your destiny; that is why you have to know God's will for your life for yourself and be careful not to look for or lean on other people's approval and opinion.

✦

Then Saul said to David, "Here is my older daughter Merab; I will give her to you as a wife. Only be valiant for me, and fight the Lord's battles." For Saul thought, "Let my hand not be against him, but let the hand of the Philistines be against him."

So David said to Saul, "Who am I, and what is my life or my father's family in Israel, that I should be son-in-law to the king?" But it happened at the time when Merab, Saul's daughter, should have been given to David, that she was given to Adriel the Meholathite as a wife.

1 SAMUEL 18:17–19 (NKJV)

Don't fight for a relationship that God never intended for you to be in because it will be a direct opposition to God's will for your life. If you are not sure about a relationship, ask God to show you. He will.

◆

I remember when I got really upset with someone I knew because, over my wife and me, they sided with a person who we all knew was a very deceitful one. I had made up my mind that I was going to confront them and tell them how wrong they were, but God stopped me. I heard God say, "Don't expect loyalty from the world when you are not of the world." So, I didn't say anything. I wanted to share this because I believe it could help someone. Many times, believers will try to be people-pleasers, and they'll want everyone to like them and be crushed when someone doesn't like them. When you take a stand with God, you stand against the world and what it believes to be right. People will have a problem with this, but it's okay as long as God is with you; that's all that matters.

"If the world hates you, you know that it hated Me before it hated you. If you were of the world, the world would love its own. Yet because you are not of the world, but I chose you out of the world, therefore the world hates you" (John 15:18–19, NKJV).

◆

"Casting down imaginations, and every high thing that exalteth itself against the knowledge of God, and bringing into captivity every thought to the obedience of Christ" (2 Corinthians 10:5, KJV).

Every thought that comes to your mind shouldn't be entertained. Thoughts that go against the Word of God need to be rebuked and cast out in

Jesus' name. Guard your mind and fill it with the Word of God because that is where the enemy attacks you.

✦

"Now when they had departed, behold, an angel of the Lord appeared to Joseph in a dream, saying, 'Arise, take the young Child and His mother, flee to Egypt, and stay there until I bring you word; for Herod will seek the young Child to destroy Him'" (Matthew 2:13, NKJV).

The young boy Jesus wasn't aware of the dangers that He faced, but Mary and Joseph did. When Herod wanted the boy dead, they took Jesus to Egypt and got Him out of harm's way. We don't know the dangers that we could have been in that God steered us away from.

Jesus was only a boy, and yet a king opposed him. I just imagined a married couple and their son versus a king and his army. Naturally, they couldn't defeat an army out of their strength, but God, simply revealing the enemy's plans and giving them direction to avoid it, spoiled the plot against them.

Not every battle is fought head-on. If we follow God's direction, we will constantly win battles we didn't even know were there. Would you instead be rescued from the enemy's clutches or be steps ahead of him? Follow God's lead, and He will keep you ahead of your enemies.

CHAPTER 7
Ministering

"Son of man, I have made you a watchman for the house of Israel; therefore hear a word from My mouth, and give them warning from Me" (Ezekiel 3:17, NKJV).

Reading this scripture reminds me of a young lady I used to go to church with. She was always upbeat, happy, and smiling. This one Sunday in particular, she looked very sad and barely spoke. At the end of the service, she came to the front and shared what was bothering her.

She told a story of a male friend she had run into earlier in the week. As they were talking and catching up, she felt God put it in her heart to speak to him about the gospel and his need to be saved. She said she was nervous and didn't want to get embarrassed, so she didn't. A few days later, her friend was shot and killed.

Whenever God puts it in your heart to minister to someone and pray for them, please don't resist it. You never know; you could be the last thing standing in between them and hell. Let God use you to destroy the enemy's plans for other people's lives.

✦

Then one of the criminals who were hanged blasphemed Him, saying, "If You are the Christ, save Yourself and us."

But the other, answering, rebuked him, saying, "Do you not even fear God, seeing you are under the same condemnation? And we indeed justly, for we receive the due reward of our deeds; but this Man has done nothing wrong." Then he said to Jesus, "Lord, remember me when You come into Your kingdom."

And Jesus said to him, "Assuredly, I say to you, today you will be with Me in Paradise."

LUKE 23:39–43 (NKJV)

Jesus was in excruciating pain, but he didn't neglect to hear this man's plea for mercy and save His soul. Jesus was dying yet fulfilling God's will. God is not willing that any perish, but that all should come to repentance (2 Peter 3:9). John 3:17 (NKJV) says, "For God did not send His Son into the world to condemn the world, but that the world through Him might be saved." Jesus is suffering and working at the same time. When we are going through hell, we cannot neglect what God has called us to do because there are souls at stake. There is still work that needs to be done. A kingdom that needs to be advanced.

✦

> And seeing the man who had been healed standing with them, they could say nothing against it. But when they had commanded them to go aside out of the council, they conferred among themselves, saying, "What shall we do to these men? For, indeed, that a notable miracle has been done through them is evident to all who dwell in Jerusalem, and we cannot deny it. But so that it spreads no further among the people, let us severely threaten them, that from now on they speak to no man in this name."

> ACTS 4:14–17 (NKJV)

The devil cannot stop God, so he'll try and stop man from speaking about God. The enemy wants to destroy God's credibility by discrediting those who represent Him. Guard yourself against the tricks of the enemy, so we represent the God we serve properly.

✦

"But I discipline my body and bring it into subjection, lest, when I have preached to others, I myself should become disqualified" (1 Corinthians 9:27, NKJV).

Those that minister the gospel need God as much as the people they are ministering to. Don't let ministry keep you so busy to the point that you don't have the time to seek God for yourself.

✦

"He said to me, 'You are my servant, Israel, in whom I will display my splendor'" (Isaiah 49:3, NIV).

God wants to show His distinctive attributes through you to the world so that He may be glorified.

✦

"So now, go. I am sending you to Pharaoh to bring my people the Israelites out of Egypt" (Exodus 3:10, NIV).

God wants to send His people to help lead others out of the darkness.

✦

"Then Peter said, 'Silver or gold I do not have, but what I do have I give you'" (Acts 3:6, NIV).

You have something on the inside of you that is more valuable than money and that people need. People need your humor and creativity. People need your warm kindness and wise advice. People are in need of your gifts and talents. God has placed things on the inside of you that can be a blessing to others.

✦

"And suddenly, a woman who had a flow of blood for twelve years came from behind and touched the hem of His garment. For she said to herself, 'If only I may touch His garment, I shall be made well'" (Matthew 9:20–21, NKJV).

"But Jesus said, 'Somebody touched Me, for I perceived power going out from Me'" (Luke 8:46, NKJV).

We are the hem of Jesus' garment because we are the vessels God's power flows through.

✦

"And this report about Him went throughout all Judea and all the surrounding region" (Luke 7:17, NKJV).

What report of God are you helping to spread across your region?

✦

"And this is eternal life, that they may know You, the only true God, and Jesus Christ whom You have sent" (John 17:3, NKJV).

Life isn't all about school, work, and paying bills. Life is about knowing God through His son Jesus Christ, and it is in a relationship with God that you find true purpose in life.

✦

"See then that you walk circumspectly, not as fools but as wise, redeeming the time, because the days are evil" (Ephesians 5:15–16, NKJV).

Now more than ever, should we be redeeming our time, not wasting it but taking every opportunity to seek and serve God.

✦

A criminal can be die-hard for a cause that he knows can lead to prison or death. How much more should we as believers be die-hard for the cause of Christ? Knowing that it will lead us to eternal life in the presence of Almighty God.

✦

Now as Jesus passed by, He saw a man who was blind from birth. And His disciples asked Him, saying, "Rabbi, who sinned, this man or his parents, that he was born blind?" Jesus answered, "Neither this man nor his parents sinned, but that the works of God should be revealed in him."

JOHN 9:1–3 (NKJV)

We are all different, but what we all have in common is that we were created so that our lives would bring glory to God.

✦

One morning I got up and knocked on my stepdad's bedroom door to ask for money to buy cereal. I told him what I wanted, and he tossed a bill down the stairs. When I picked it up, I realized that it was only a piece of a ten-dollar bill. I went upstairs and showed him what he had given to me, and he reached in his pocket, found the other piece, and handed it to me. The look on my face must have shown him that I didn't want it because he said, "That money still spends." I found some tape, put the bill back together as best I could, and went to the store. The whole time I was worried that the bill would be rejected. While at the store, I grabbed cereal and a gallon of milk and got in line. I was nervous, not knowing if the money was even worth something.

The cashier scanned the milk and cereal and gave me the total. I handed her the patched-up bill looking intently at her face to see how she would react. She took it and gave me my change. Before she even noticed that it was torn, she recognized it for what it was. I realized being damaged didn't take away the fact that it was still a ten-dollar bill. It still had value. People may struggle, make bad decisions, and their lives may be falling apart, but they are still people. They still matter. Before people pass judgment on someone for their problems, they should first see them for who they are—a human being. They are valuable, and they are worth something. Like the torn ten-dollar bill, a person still has purpose despite the condition they are in. People's lives can be restored and renewed in the hands of God. We just have to tell the world what God is capable of and share what He's done in our lives for people to believe.

✦

"In him was life, and that life was the light of all mankind" (John 1:4, NIV).

Let us not hold back the light within us when people in darkness need it. As believers, if we don't tell people about the light (Jesus Christ), how will they see it?

✦

"And this gospel of the kingdom will be preached in all the world as a witness to all the nations, and then the end will come" (Matthew 24:14, NKJV).

No one knows when the end will come, but the determining factor is spreading the gospel around the whole world. Jesus Himself doesn't even know when He is returning, so why would we?

"But of that day and hour no one knows, not even the angels of heaven, but My Father only" (Matthew 24:36, NKJV).

If Jesus did know, you can imagine that we would also because He would've told us based on this scripture.

"No longer do I call you servants, for a servant does not know what his master is doing; but I have called you friends, for all things that I heard from My Father I have made known to you" (John 15:15, NKJV).

✦

"This is what the Lord says: 'Let not the wise boast of their wisdom or the strong boast of their strength or the rich boast of their riches'" (Jeremiah 9:23, NIV).

People boast about their wisdom, strength, and riches out of pride, even though these all come with limitations. Since God has no limits and can make the impossible possible, how much more should we boast about God out of our reverence for Him?

"'But let the one who boasts boast about this: that they have the understanding to know me, that I am the Lord, who exercises kindness, justice and righteousness on earth, for in these I delight,' declares the Lord" (Jeremiah 9:24, NIV).

✦

"Now it came to pass, afterward, that He went through every city and village, preaching and bringing the glad tidings of the kingdom of God. And the twelve were with Him" (Luke 8:1, NKJV).

Everywhere that Jesus went, He spoke encouraging words that would change the mood of the environment He was in. People may have been down and discouraged, but when Jesus came, He brought them joy and peace through the Word of God. As believers, with the spirit of God on the inside of us, when we come in contact with people who have no hope, we can speak life into them and bring comfort to their souls.

"Therefore, of these men who have accompanied us all the time that the Lord Jesus went in and out among us, beginning from the baptism of John to that day when He was taken up from us, one of these must become a witness with us of His resurrection" (Acts 1:21–22, NKJV).

Based on this scripture, the twelve disciples weren't the only ones Jesus discipled. There were others that walked with Jesus and witnessed His ministry firsthand that aren't mentioned by name. It's safe to say that they also went out into the world and preached the gospel.

Many people in the Body of Christ won't have a big platform, be famous or pastor a church. They will be unknown to most people, but the work that God gives them to do will be just as important. Some people will make a significant impact on the world, and we won't hear about them.

"For the kingdom of heaven is like a man traveling to a far country, who called his own servants and delivered his goods to them. [...] But he who had received one went and dug in the ground, and hid his lord's money" (Matthew 25:14, 18, NKJV).

Digging a hole isn't an easy task; it takes time and energy. You will waste time and exhaust yourself by running from what God has called you to do. Be faithful to what God has entrusted to you. Put your gifts and talents that God has given you to work and bring Him glory.

Sometimes we encounter people that have been through so much that they are ready to give up. We can pray that God helps lift them up so that they can gain strength to keep going and place their trust in God.

"And they stood up in their place and read from the Book of the Law of the Lord their God for one-fourth of the day; and for another fourth they confessed and worshiped the Lord their God" (Nehemiah 9:3, NKJV).

In the Old Testament, the preacher would preach for six hours. Then they would do praising, worshipping, and confessing for another six hours. And people today think that an hour service is too long.

"'Come, follow me,' Jesus said, 'and I will send you out to fish for people.' At once they left their nets and followed him" (Matthew 4:19–20, NIV).

Notice how fast they responded to what Jesus said. We should be quick to move when God tells us to move. Don't let procrastination hold you back from the work God wants you to do.

"Then He said to them, 'The harvest truly is great, but the laborers are few; therefore pray the Lord of the harvest to send out laborers into His harvest'" (Luke 10:2, NKJV).

This means that more people are ready to receive Jesus Christ than people are preaching Jesus Christ. We have to take the opportunities we get to minister the gospel to the lost.

> If anyone wills to do His will, he shall know concerning the doctrine, whether it is from God or whether I speak on My own authority. He who speaks from himself seeks his own glory; but He who seeks the glory of the One who sent Him is true, and no unrighteousness is in Him.
>
> JOHN 7:17–18 (NKJV)

Believers should be able to tell the difference between someone speaking true gospel on behalf of God versus someone speaking their own words on behalf of themselves. We have to discern when a person is trying to get glory for themselves while pretending to bring glory to the Lord.

"As iron sharpens iron, so one person sharpens another" (Proverbs 27:17, NIV).

People can either sharpen your faith, mind, and talents or bring dullness to it. It's not meant for you to receive from everyone.

✦

> Then an angel of the Lord appeared to him, standing at the right side of the altar of incense. When Zechariah saw him, he was startled and was gripped with fear. But the angel said to him: "Do not be afraid, Zechariah; your prayer has been heard. Your wife Elizabeth will bear you a son, and you are to call him John. He will be a joy and delight to you, and many will rejoice because of his birth, for he will be great in the sight of the Lord. He is never to take wine or other fermented drink, and he will be filled with the Holy Spirit even before he is born. He will bring back many of the people of Israel to the Lord their God. And he will go on before the Lord, in the spirit and power of Elijah, to turn the hearts of the parents to their children and the disobedient to the wisdom of the righteous—to make ready a people prepared for the Lord."
>
> LUKE 1:11–17 (NIV)

"And the child grew and became strong in spirit; and he lived in the wilderness until he appeared publicly to Israel" (Luke 1:80, NIV).

The life of John the Baptist is pretty interesting. John didn't have much; he lived with the bare minimum. The Bible doesn't say anything about him having a home or shelter in the wilderness. The Bible doesn't mention him having an animal to ride. John didn't wear nice clothes. He wore camel's hair. John didn't eat the best of foods: his main course was locust. He also ate wild honey. Where there is wild honey, there are wild bees, so you can only imagine what he had to go through to get that. Imagine someone trying to give you advice for your life, and they ate cockroaches, syrup, and wore dog's hair for clothing. Most people would avoid a person like that and say they're crazy. I'm pretty sure this is how John the Baptist was viewed, but people still were drawn to him. John still brought people closer to God. People can make the mistake of thinking that for them to do a work for God, everything has to look extravagant to be effective and for people to come. They have to have the latest technology and amazing-looking building. If God is with you, if you are anointed, and you have a Word from God, that's all you need.

When the messengers of John had departed, He began to speak

to the multitudes concerning John: "What did you go out into the wilderness to see? A reed shaken by the wind? But what did you go out to see? A man clothed in soft garments? Indeed those who are gorgeously appareled and live in luxury are in kings' courts. But what did you go out to see? A prophet? Yes, I say to you, and more than a prophet."

LUKE 7:24–26 (NKJV)

John the Baptist didn't have much, but it was all he needed to complete God's plan for his life. His purpose was to prepare a way for the Lord, and he did that. He did it while living in the wilderness. While living in rough conditions. Can a person really have an excuse for why they cannot do what God created them to do?

"While Paul was waiting for them in Athens, he was greatly distressed to see that the city was full of idols. So he reasoned in the synagogue with both Jews and God-fearing Greeks, as well as in the marketplace day by day with those who happened to be there" (Acts 17:16–17, NIV).

Paul was sad to see that the people were putting their trust in lifeless statues that couldn't do anything for them. He felt obligated to tell people about Jesus, the only one who could save their souls. We daily come in contact with people whose lives are filled with idols, and we must tell them about the one true living God who alone is trustworthy.

In the meantime His disciples urged Him, saying, "Rabbi, eat." But He said to them, "I have food to eat of which you do not know." Therefore the disciples said to one another, "Has anyone brought Him anything to eat?" Jesus said to them, "My food is to do the will of Him who sent Me, and to finish His work."

JOHN 4:31–34 (NKJV)

Living outside of God's will causes people to feel an empty void. Walking in God's plan and purpose for your life will bring true satisfaction and fulfillment. Doing what God created you to do will satisfy your soul the same way good food satisfies your natural body.

"For God did not send His Son into the world to condemn the world, but that the world through Him might be saved" (John 3:17, NKJV).

When God sends a man or woman of God, it's never to bring condemnation to people. They may give correction, but their main objective is to speak life, not condemn.

"And the disciples came and said to Him, 'Why do You speak to them in parables?' He answered and said to them, 'Because it has been given to you to know the mysteries of the kingdom of heaven, but to them it has not been given'" (Matthew 13:10–11, NKJV).

Jesus spoke in parables to get people to understand the spiritual truth of God's Word. He used the natural to get people to understand the spiritual.

You can be discouraged, and God will use you to encourage someone else. You can feel down, and God will use you to help lift someone up. We can't allow what we are going through to stop us from ministering to people. God is going to take care of our needs, but in the meantime, there are souls that need to be saved and plans of the devil that need to be destroyed.

"My dear brothers and sisters, take note of this: Everyone should be quick to listen, slow to speak and slow to become angry" (James 1:19, NIV).

It's not always about being heard but taking the time to hear others.

"Now when Peter had come to Antioch, I withstood him to his face, because he was to be blamed; for before certain men came from James, he would eat with the Gentiles; but when they came, he withdrew and separated himself, fearing those who were of the circumcision" (Galatians 2:11–12, NKJV).

The Bible tells believers how to deal with conflict between one another. God doesn't tell us to act like we don't have a problem with someone when there is one. Instead of harboring negative feelings towards someone or even gossiping about them, God would rather you go to them to resolve the issue.

"Moreover if your brother sins against you, go and tell him his fault between you and him alone. If he hears you, you have gained your brother" (Matthew 18:15, NKJV).

Just because we are believers doesn't mean we won't disagree. Even the twelve disciples disagreed. If we wrong someone, we can repent. If we have been wronged, we can forgive. When offenses within the Body of Christ go unresolved, it can lead to bitterness, unforgiveness, and division. Imagine how many broken relationships there are due to misunderstandings and lack of communication. There is a reason God commanded us to love one another because He wants unity amongst His children.

While at work, I started to have this really intense craving for fried chicken. Believe it or not, it was odd for me because usually, chicken is not at the top of my list of things to eat when I get hungry. I sent my mom a text asking where I should go to get some, and she told me Popeyes. As I was driving, I felt it was not by chance that I was going to this place but that I was being led. The GPS took me to a part of town that I was familiar with but hadn't been to in a very long time. I hadn't eaten at the place in years. I walked in, glanced around, and made my way to the counter. After staring at the menu, I decided what to eat and placed my order. "Is this for here or to go?" the cashier asked. "For here." I sat down at a table by the door while waiting for my food.

The feeling that I had been sent got stronger, so I looked around to see who I had been sent there for. Not too long after I sat down, a man outside caught my eye. I watched him through the window as he came inside. He asked if he could sit down at the table, and of course, I said "yes." He asked if I read the Bible and pulled one out of his backpack. At that moment, I knew I had been led there for him.

We talked about the Word of God, and he told me how he used to walk with the Lord up until the point when he cheated on his wife and left her for the other woman. He also shared that he became homeless soon after and had been with the girl ever since. He even referenced 1 Kings 11:2, in which God warned his people not to get involved with certain women that would turn their hearts away from Him to false idols. I asked if he still felt like God was reaching out to him to bring him back into the relationships that he once had; he said, "Yes, because I'm sitting here talking to you." I asked if I could pray for him, and he said "yes."

After praying, I opened my eyes to see tears coming down his face. He thanked me, then got up and left. My number was called, so I got up, grabbed my food, and sat back down to eat. I smiled, finding it funny that God would use my appetite to place me in a position to minister to a lost soul.

"Remind them of these things, charging them before the Lord not to strive about words to no profit, to the ruin of the hearers" (2 Timothy 2:14, NKJV).

It's best to pray that God opens the eyes of people who are blind to the truth and argumentative. Arguing with them will only wear you out, frustrate you and steal your peace. Sometimes it's not always meant for you to engage but to pray.

> Then Jesus answered and said: "A certain man went down from Jerusalem to Jericho, and fell among thieves, who stripped him of his clothing, wounded him, and departed, leaving him half dead. […] But a certain Samaritan, as he journeyed, came where he was. And when he saw him, he had compassion. So he went to him and bandaged his wounds, pouring on oil and wine; and he set him on his own animal, brought him to an inn, and took care of him."
>
> LUKE 10:30, 33–34 (NKJV)

We need more good Samaritans in the world. People that God can place in the path of someone wounded who will assist in their healing process.

People shouldn't use the pulpit to air out their grievances. The pulpit is not the place to take shots at those you are having problems with. People come to hear the Word of God, not a rant. Take the pettiness out of the preaching.

CHAPTER 8

Sweet Salvation and the Holy Spirit

"Nor is there salvation in any other, for there is no other name under heaven given among men by which we must be saved" (Acts 4:12, NKJV).

A true believer, a faithful follower of Jesus Christ, would not accept, acknowledge or agree that there are other ways to God. According to scripture, there is no other way.

"Jesus said to him, 'I am the way, the truth, and the life. No one comes to the Father except through Me'" (John 14:6, NKJV).

✦

"And it shall come to pass That whoever calls on the name of the Lord Shall be saved" (Acts 2:21, NKJV).

Whoever—anyone, any person, whoever wants it. Your background, race, or current condition doesn't matter, and salvation is for everyone. It is not exclusive to one particular group of people.

✦

"All that the Father gives Me will come to Me, and the one who comes to Me I will by no means cast out" (John 6:37, NKJV).

The Lord turns away no one who wants Him in their life.

✦

Now while they were going, behold, some of the guard came into the city and reported to the chief priests all the things that had happened. When they had assembled with the elders and consulted together, they gave a large sum of money to the soldiers, saying, "Tell them, 'His disciples came at night and stole Him away while we slept.' […]" So they took the money and did as they were instructed; and this saying is commonly reported among the Jews until this day.

MATTHEW 28:11–13, 15 (NKJV)

The religious leaders knew about Jesus resurrecting from the dead because the soldiers who guarded His tomb told them what happened. Instead of admitting that they had been wrong about Jesus, they attempted to cover up His resurrection.

Some people can be so stubborn-hearted that they refuse to accept what they know to be true and continue living a lie that benefits them more. Let's pray that God softens the hearts of people so that they can receive Jesus Christ.

✦

"Rather, as it is written: 'Those who were not told about him will see, and those who have not heard will understand'" (Romans 15:21, NIV).

Everyone will get a chance to receive Jesus Christ as Lord and Savior.

✦

"As Jesus passed on from there, He saw a man named Matthew sitting at the tax office. And He said to him, 'Follow Me.' So he arose and followed Him" (Matthew 9:9, NKJV).

In biblical times, tax collectors were considered the scum of the earth. Fellow Jews working for the Roman government, oppressing and stealing from their people. It was said that tax collectors would set the taxes higher than usual to get a cut.

So, Matthew is in the middle of sinning, and Jesus calls out to him. While he's sinning, Jesus offers him salvation, and Matthew accepts. This is what it means to come as you are. Even in our fallen state, God wants us. Matthew gets up and leaves his old lifestyle behind to follow Jesus.

✦

"Now it happened, the day after, that He went into a city called Nain; and many of His disciples went with Him, and a large crowd" (Luke 7:11, NKJV).

Many times, the Bible talks about the crowds that were around Jesus and His disciples. There is a difference between the two. The disciples are committed to Jesus and follow Him, and the crowds are around just to see what's going on and want to benefit from Jesus.

✦

"Therefore I say to you, her sins, which are many, are forgiven, for she loved much. But to whom little is forgiven, the same loves little" (Luke 7:47, NKJV).

People who have been counted out and viewed as the worst of sinners become some of the most committed and active children of God once they're saved.

✦

"A sower went out to sow his seed. And as he sowed, some fell by the wayside; and it was trampled down, and the birds of the air devoured it. Some fell on rock; and as soon as it sprang up, it withered away because it lacked moisture. And some fell among thorns, and the thorns sprang up with it and choked it. But others fell on good ground, sprang up, and yielded a crop a hundredfold." When He had said these things He cried, "He who has ears to hear, let him hear!"

LUKE 8:5–8 (NKJV)

Believers are the sowers, and the seed is the Word of God. If we never sow seed (share the word), we'll never see it take root and grow (lead people to Christ).

✦

"Surely the arm of the Lord is not too short to save, nor his ear too dull to hear" (Isaiah 59:1, NIV).

No one is too far gone to where God can't reach them when they call out to Him.

✦

Now Jesus sat opposite the treasury and saw how the people put money into the treasury. And many who were rich put in much. Then one poor widow came and threw in two mites, which make a quadrans. So He called His disciples to Himself and said to them, "Assuredly, I say to you that this poor widow has put in more than all those who have given to the treasury; for they all put in out of their abundance, but she out of her poverty put in all that she had, her whole livelihood."

MARK 12:41–44 (NKJV)

This woman didn't have much, but she gave all she had. You may not have much in your bank account, and you may not own a lot of material things. But the question is, are you giving God your all? Are you all in with God? Are you giving Him your obedience? Are you giving Him reverence and honor? Are you giving Him your time? Or are you holding back?

✦

Committing a sin, feeling conviction, and repenting is different from living in sin, being comfortable, and using God's grace to justify it.

✦

"Also for Adam and his wife the Lord God made tunics of skin, and clothed them" (Genesis 3:21, NKJV).

After Adam and Eve sinned against God in the garden and had to leave, God made them clothes to wear. It's amazing that even if we fall short and sin, God will still cover us. God still cares, and He is still concerned for us, and that is love.

✦

"For you died, and your life is hidden with Christ in God" (Colossians 3:3, NKJV).

With all the danger in the world that we live in, the safest place to be is in Christ.

✦

"By faith Moses, when he became of age, refused to be called the son of Pharaoh's daughter, choosing rather to suffer affliction with the people of God than to enjoy the passing pleasures of sin" (Hebrews 11:24–25, NKJV).

Moses lived a lavish lifestyle, being adopted by the daughter of Pharaoh, king of Egypt. He was a part of one of the wealthiest and most powerful families in the world. Moses was well respected and likely feared. He could have anything he wanted. But when he found out that he was a Hebrew, a race of people Pharaoh had decided to enslave, he sided with them. When God spoke to Moses and revealed His will for his life, he accepted it and went against the people who took him in. He chose to suffer as a man of God rather than live it up as Pharaoh's grandson. Moses knew that his relationship with God was more valuable than anything that the world had to offer. Treasure your relationship with God and know that there is nothing more precious.

✦

After the death of Moses the servant of the Lord, it came to pass that the Lord spoke to Joshua the son of Nun, Moses' assistant, saying: "Moses My servant is dead. Now therefore, arise, go over this Jordan, you and all this people, to the land which I am giving to them—the children of Israel"

JOSHUA 1:1–2 (NKJV)

Your identity and purpose should never be found in another person. If it is, what happens when that person hurts you, rejects you, or passes away? Notice when Moses died, God didn't waste any time in choosing Joshua to continue His work. Man will die, but God will live forever. Our purpose, identity, and destiny are in God, so we should never try to find it or place it in anything other than Him.

✦

When Jesus reached the spot, he looked up and said to him, "Zacchaeus, come down immediately. I must stay at your house today."

So he came down at once and welcomed him gladly.

All the people saw this and began to mutter, "He has gone to be the guest of a sinner."

But Zacchaeus stood up and said to the Lord, "Look, Lord! Here and now I give half of my possessions to the poor, and if I have cheated anybody out of anything, I will pay back four times the amount."

Jesus said to him, "Today salvation has come to this house, because this man, too, is a son of Abraham."

LUKE 19:5–9 (NIV)

Jesus goes to the home of Zacchaeus, who the church avoids because he is a sinner. While Jesus is there, Zacchaeus becomes convicted of his sin and repents. People live ungodly lives when God is absent in their life. For some people, all they need is to experience God's presence, which will cause them to want to change, repent, and live for God.

✦

Now the whole earth had one language and one speech. And it came to pass, as they journeyed from the east, that they found a plain in the land of Shinar, and they dwelt there. Then they said to one another, "Come, let us make bricks and bake them thoroughly." They had brick for stone, and they had asphalt for mortar. And they said, "Come, let us build ourselves a city, and a tower whose top is in the heavens; let us make a name for ourselves, lest we be scattered abroad over the face of the whole earth."

GENESIS 11:1–4 (NKJV)

The building of the tower of Babel is man's attempt to get to heaven.
"For it is by grace you have been saved, through faith—and this is not from yourselves, it is the gift of God—not by works, so that no one can boast" (Ephesians 2:8–9, NIV).
　　The only way to heaven is through faith in Jesus Christ.

✦

"In the beginning God created the heavens and the earth. The earth was without form, and void; and darkness was on the face of the deep. And the Spirit of God was hovering over the face of the waters" (Genesis 1:1–2, NKJV).
　　Before God began to work on the earth, it had no foundation, and it was void. This is similar to how a person's life is before God's work of salvation through faith in Jesus Christ. Also, notice that God didn't have to create darkness. Darkness is present where God is absent, and He alone has the authority and power to drive it out.

✦

"And I will pray the Father, and He will give you another Helper, that He may abide with you forever" (John 14:16, NKJV).
　　Jesus sent the Holy Spirit to help us.

✦

"For He whom God has sent speaks the words of God, for God does not give the Spirit by measure" (John 3:34, NKJV).
　　The Holy Spirit relays information from God to us. We can also receive as much of the Holy Spirit as we want.

"Now the Lord is the Spirit; and where the Spirit of the Lord is, there is liberty" (2 Corinthians 3:17, NKJV).

The Holy Spirit brings freedom into the atmosphere when He is present.

"But you shall receive power when the Holy Spirit has come upon you; and you shall be witnesses to Me in Jerusalem, and in all Judea and Samaria, and to the end of the earth" (Acts 1:8, NKJV).

The Holy Spirit empowers us to do God's will.

"Paul and his companions traveled throughout the region of Phrygia and Galatia, having been kept by the Holy Spirit from preaching the word in the province of Asia" (Acts 16:6, NIV).

The Holy Spirit can keep you from places God doesn't want you to be.

"For who knows a person's thoughts except their own spirit within them? In the same way no one knows the thoughts of God except the Spirit of God" (1 Corinthians 2:11, NIV).

The Holy Spirit can reveal God's thoughts to you.

"So he came by the Spirit into the temple" (Luke 2:27, NKJV).

The Holy Spirit can lead you to a place God predestined for you to be so His will can be done there.

"And it had been revealed to him by the Holy Spirit that he would not see death before he had seen the Lord's Christ" (Luke 2:26, NKJV).

The Holy Spirit can reveal the future to you.

"Now it is God who makes both us and you stand firm in Christ. He anointed us, set his seal of ownership on us, and put his Spirit in our hearts as a deposit, guaranteeing what is to come" (2 Corinthians 1:21–22, NIV).

God has given His people the Holy Spirit as a deposit. With all the power we have on the inside, there is no reason we shouldn't be productive for God.

The Spirit of God is active, and we should allow the Holy Spirit to act through us. Let us give God a good return on His investment and be profitable to His kingdom.

◆

"Nicodemus answered and said to Him, 'How can these things be?' Jesus answered and said to him, 'Are you the teacher of Israel, and do not know these things?'" (John 3:9–10, NKJV).

Nicodemus was familiar with scripture but didn't have revelation. The Holy Spirit can show us what our natural minds cannot comprehend, giving us in-depth knowledge and understanding from God's word.

"But God has revealed them to us through His Spirit. For the Spirit searches all things, yes, the deep things of God" (1 Corinthians 2:10, NKJV).

◆

And when they had set them in the midst, they asked, "By what power or by what name have you done this?"

Then Peter, filled with the Holy Spirit, said to them, "Rulers of the people and elders of Israel: [...] let it be known to you all, and to all the people of Israel, that by the name of Jesus Christ of Nazareth, whom you crucified, whom God raised from the dead, by Him this man stands here before you whole. [...] Nor is there salvation in any other, for there is no other name under heaven given among men by which we must be saved."

ACTS 4:7–8, 10, 12 (NKJV)

This is the first time since Peter's denial that he's being questioned, and the answer that he gives could reveal his connection to Jesus Christ. Instead of lying again in an attempt to avoid persecution and save himself—remember that Matthew 16:25 (NKJV) says, "For whoever desires to save his life will lose it, but whoever loses his life for My sake will find it,"—Peter boldly confesses that Jesus Christ is Lord.

"Now when they saw the boldness of Peter and John, and perceived that they were uneducated and untrained men, they marveled. And they realized that they had been with Jesus" (Acts 4:13, NKJV).

What changed? What was different about him now than before? The difference is now Peter is filled with the Holy Spirit. There is boldness that comes with the Holy Spirit. God is not a coward, and we shouldn't be either. We can tap into a courageous boldness that's available to us through the Holy Spirit. Yes, we may experience fear, because the enemy wants us to, but we don't have to be controlled by it. The religious leaders perceived that Peter and John were uneducated and untrained men because they didn't school them. When it comes to the things of God, the Holy Spirit can educate and train you in ways a school cannot.

"Nevertheless I tell you the truth. It is to your advantage that I go away; for if I do not go away, the Helper will not come to you; but if I depart, I will send Him to you. And when He has come, He will convict the world of sin, and of righteousness, and of judgment" (John 16:7–8, NKJV).

Jesus said it was to their advantage that He go away and the Holy Spirit comes. Having the Holy Spirit inside of you gives you an advantage in life. Also, the Holy Spirit's job is to bring conviction that leads to repentance. When man tries to do the Holy Spirit's job, it can be condemning.

"I will put My Spirit within you and cause you to walk in My statutes, and you will keep My judgments and do them" (Ezekiel 36:27, NKJV).

No one can serve God out of their own strength and ability. It is the Holy Spirit that God gives His people that enables them to live for Him.

"Now hope does not disappoint, because the love of God has been poured out in our hearts by the Holy Spirit who was given to us" (Romans 5:5, NKJV).

In a world where love is lacking, let God show His love to people through you. In fact, love is an indicator that you are a disciple of Jesus Christ.

"A new command I give you: Love one another. As I have loved you, so you must love one another. By this everyone will know that you are my disciples, if you love one another" (John 13:34–35, NIV).

✦

"You are of God, little children, and have overcome them, because He who is in you is greater than he who is in the world" (1 John 4:4, NKJV).

As a believer, there is power inside you to overcome anything that the world throws at you.

✦

"And they overcame him by the blood of the Lamb and by the word of their testimony" (Revelation 12:11, NKJV).

Your testimony is a weapon against the devil. By sharing it, you are destroying the lies of the enemy by showing people that God is real. God can save. God can heal. God can deliver. God can transform them into the person He created them to be. Their life can change. Never underestimate the power of your testimony.

CHAPTER 9

Leadership

"So I took the leading men of your tribes, wise and respected men, and appointed them to have authority over you—as commanders of thousands, of hundreds, of fifties and of tens and as tribal officials" (Deuteronomy 1:15, NIV).

Notice it didn't say Moses took men that were licensed and educated. He took men that were respected. You can have the knowledge, but what kind of impression have you left amongst the people? Do they trust you? Do they sense you are genuine and have the love of God in your heart?

We see that these commanders are placed over different amounts of people. It's because some could handle tens but not fifties, and some could handle fifties but not hundreds. Some could handle hundreds but not thousands. God knows who can handle what. He said He would not put more on you than you can bear.

✦

At Gibeon the Lord appeared to Solomon in a dream by night; and God said, "Ask! What shall I give you?"

And Solomon said: "You have shown great mercy to Your servant David my father, because he walked before You in truth, in righteousness, and in uprightness of heart with You; You have continued this great kindness for him, and You have given him a son to sit on his throne, as it is this day. Now, O Lord my God, You have made Your servant king instead of my father David, but I am a little child; I do not know how to go out or come in. And Your servant is in the midst of Your people whom You have chosen, a great people, too numerous to be numbered or counted. Therefore give to Your servant an understanding heart to judge Your people, that I may discern between good and evil. For who is able to judge this great people of Yours?"

The speech pleased the Lord, that Solomon had asked this thing. Then God said to him: "Because you have asked this thing, and have not asked long life for yourself, nor have asked riches for yourself, nor have asked the life of your enemies, but have asked for yourself understanding to discern justice, behold,

I have done according to your words; see, I have given you a wise and understanding heart, so that there has not been anyone like you before you, nor shall any like you arise after you."

1 KINGS 3:5–12 (NKJV)

God gave king Solomon wisdom to manage a kingdom and lead a nation of people. God can give you the wisdom to manage your home and lead your family, and all you have to do is ask for it.

"If any of you lacks wisdom, let him ask of God, who gives to all liberally and without reproach, and it will be given to him" (James 1:5, NKJV).

✦

"Let no one despise your youth, but be an example to the believers in word, in conduct, in love, in spirit, in faith, in purity" (1 Timothy 4:12, NKJV).

Believers should not only be an example to the world but also be an example to other believers.

✦

"And He came down with them and stood on a level place with a crowd of His disciples and a great multitude of people from all Judea and Jerusalem, and from the seacoast of Tyre and Sidon, who came to hear Him and be healed of their diseases" (Luke 6:17, NKJV).

The part I want to focus on is where it says He "stood on a level place" with the crowd. Jesus didn't put Himself above the people and looked down on them. Jesus was a man of the people. A man or woman of God should not pridefully exalt themselves. Leaders are servants first.

"Just as the Son of Man did not come to be served, but to serve, and to give His life a ransom for many" (Matthew 20:28, NKJV).

All believers have essential roles in the Body of Christ, and no one is more valuable than the next person. Like Paul said, let us not think more highly of ourselves than we ought to (Romans 12:3).

✦

"When these things were accomplished, Paul purposed in the Spirit, when he had passed through Macedonia and Achaia, to go to Jerusalem, saying, 'After I have been there, I must also see Rome'" (Acts 19:21, NKJV).

The part I want to highlight is where it says, "Paul purposed in the Spirit." Do you make plans that are in line with the Spirit of God or your flesh?

✦

"Now the man Moses was very humble, more than all men who were on the face of the earth" (Numbers 12:3, NKJV).

For Moses to be the humblest man on earth, he had to have been extremely humble, and this is why God chose Moses to be a leader and lead the people of Israel out of Egypt.

"And whoever exalts himself will be humbled, and he who humbles himself will be exalted" (Matthew 23:12, NKJV).

✦

"Then He commanded His disciples that they should tell no one that He was Jesus the Christ" (Matthew 16:20, NKJV).

We live in a world where everyone wants to be known. People love recognition and attention. If you notice, Jesus never went out of His way to prove to people who He was. He let His actions speak for Him, and we should too. Let your walk with God speak for you.

"The Jews who were there gathered around him, saying, 'How long will you keep us in suspense? If you are the Messiah, tell us plainly.' Jesus answered, 'I did tell you, but you do not believe. The works I do in my Father's name testify about me'" (John 10:24–25, NIV).

✦

Now Korah the son of Izhar, the son of Kohath, the son of Levi, with Dathan and Abiram the sons of Eliab, and On the son of Peleth, sons of Reuben, took men; and they rose up before Moses with some of the children of Israel, two hundred and fifty leaders of the congregation, representatives of the congregation, men of renown. They gathered together against Moses and Aaron, and said to them, "You take too much upon yourselves, for all the congregation is holy, every one of them, and the Lord is among them. Why then do you exalt yourselves above the assembly of the Lord?"

NUMBERS 16:1–3 (NKJV)

The very people that Moses helped lead out of Egypt turned on him. Moses fought for them, was there for them when they had trouble, and loved them. Yet, they still had a problem with him being their leader and wanted to take his place. In some instances, no matter how good you are to certain people, it won't change the fact that they aren't for you because they want what you have.

✦

"So it was, as they were burying a man, that suddenly they spied a band of raiders; and they put the man in the tomb of Elisha; and when the man was let down and touched the bones of Elisha, he revived and stood on his feet" (2 Kings 13:21, NKJV).

I want to have the kind of impact Elisha had on people that came in contact with him. He lived such a godly life that he still brought life to people in dead situations even long after he passed away.

✦

"But there was a certain man called Simon, who previously practiced sorcery in the city and astonished the people of Samaria, claiming that he was someone great" (Acts 8:9, NKJV).

This man practiced witchcraft, and he was known to put himself on a pedestal above the people to glorify himself. If someone is in the pulpit and boasting about who they are, what they have, and what they've done, they are basically trying to bring glory to themselves, which is what people who practice witchcraft do.

✦

For the kingdom of heaven is like a man traveling to a far country, who called his own servants and delivered his goods to them. And to one he gave five talents, to another two, and to another one, to each according to his own ability; and immediately he went on a journey.

MATTHEW 25:14–15 (NKJV)

When I read this, I'm surprised that the servants didn't get into an argument over who got what. The servant with the one talent wasn't jealous of the servant who got two. The servant with two talents wasn't jealous of the one that got five.

These servants weren't worried about each other. There was no envy. We have no say-so in what God gives to the next person. You may not have a certain gift; you may not have a certain anointing, but what are you doing with what you do have? People can lose their identity by comparing themselves to other people. Don't try to measure up to the next person; be who God made you to be. Only you can be you.

For the servant who got five talents, the Bible says that from whom much is given, much is required (Luke 12:48). He had more responsibility than the others, but God gave him the grace to handle it. Don't try and take on something God didn't give you the grace to handle. The Bible says that God will not put more on you than you can bear, but sometimes we put more on ourselves when we try to be someone we are not.

✦

"For even the Son of Man did not come to be served, but to serve, and to give His life a ransom for many" (Mark 10:45, NKJV).

The attitude of a leader should be, "What can I do to serve the people?" Not what should the people do to serve them.

✦

And the Lord spoke to Moses, saying, "Send men to spy out the land of Canaan, which I am giving to the children of Israel; from each tribe of their fathers you shall send a man, every one a leader among them."

[…]

Then they told him, and said: "We went to the land where you sent us. It truly flows with milk and honey, and this is its fruit. Nevertheless the people who dwell in the land are strong; the cities are fortified and very large; moreover we saw the descendants of Anak there."

NUMBERS 13:1–2, 27–28 (NKJV)

But the men who had gone up with him said, "We are not able to go up against the people, for they are stronger than we." And they gave the children of Israel a bad report of the land which they had spied out, saying, "The land through which we have gone as spies is a land that devours its inhabitants, and all the people whom we saw in it are men of great stature. There we saw the giants (the descendants of Anak came from the giants); and we were like grasshoppers in our own sight, and so we were in their sight."

NUMBERS 13:31–33 (NKJV)

The leaders of the tribes were sent to spy out the land, and they came back with a bad report. The doubt from the leaders trickled down to everyone in their tribe. Doubt is contagious. If a leader doesn't know how to trust God and take Him at His word, he shouldn't be followed. A leader should have the faith to believe God for the impossible because they are supposed to help build others' faith. We can be a stumbling block to our own brothers and sisters when we speak negatively about something they are trying to believe God for. If they had come back and spoken encouraging words of faith, they would have entered into the Promised Land. Don't hinder people from reaching their Promised Land.

✦

When they kept on questioning him, he straightened up and said to them, "Let any one of you who is without sin be the first to throw a stone at her."

Again he stooped down and wrote on the ground. At this, those who heard began to go away one at a time, the older ones first, until only Jesus was left, with the woman still standing there.

JOHN 8:7–9 (NIV)

As self-righteous as the religious leaders were, they knew they weren't perfect like they wanted people to believe.

✦

"You are still worldly. For since there is jealousy and quarreling among you, are you not worldly? Are you not acting like mere humans?" (1 Corinthians 3:3, NIV).

Jealousy and constant quarreling are signs of immaturity. Leaders are to set an example on how to be secure with who you are in Christ and how to deal with difficult people while still being Christlike.

✦

"And when it was day, He called His disciples to Himself; and from them He chose twelve whom He also named apostles" (Luke 6:13, NKJV).

We see here that it was the Lord who chose those that would be apostles, not man. It's not a position that you choose; God gives it.

✦

> And in Lystra a certain man without strength in his feet was sitting, a cripple from his mother's womb, who had never walked. This man heard Paul speaking. Paul, observing him intently and seeing that he had faith to be healed, said with a loud voice, "Stand up straight on your feet!" And he leaped and walked. Now when the people saw what Paul had done, they raised their voices, saying in the Lycaonian language, "The gods have come down to us in the likeness of men!" And Barnabas they called Zeus, and Paul, Hermes, because he was the chief speaker. Then the priest of Zeus, whose temple was in front of their city, brought oxen and garlands to the gates, intending to sacrifice with the multitudes.
> [...]
> Then Jews from Antioch and Iconium came there; and having persuaded the multitudes, they stoned Paul and dragged him out of the city, supposing him to be dead.

ACTS 14:8–13 14:19 (NKJV)

These people tried to worship Paul like he was a god, but after being persuaded by the words of Paul's opposers, they stoned him.

People can praise you one moment and then persecute you the next. People can also let the opinions of others change the way they feel toward you, when they know you better than them.

We should never live for the praise of people or allow people to idolize us. Live to give God the praise and point people to Jesus Christ. If people persecute you for doing what's right, it's okay because we live to please God, not man.

"Remember the word that I said to you, 'A servant is not greater than his master.' If they persecuted Me, they will also persecute you. If they kept My word, they will keep yours also" (John 15:20, NKJV).

✦

"Have I therefore become your enemy because I tell you the truth?" (Galatians 4:16, NKJV).

A person who truly cares for you will tell you the truth, out of love, whether you want to hear it or not. It's easy for someone to lie to you when they don't have your best interest at heart. We should honor the honesty in those around us and not become offensive when they are honest about us being in error. No one is always right; it's okay to receive correction, and it doesn't make you less of a believer or leader.

✦

"Train up a child in the way he should go, And when he is old he will not depart from it" (Proverbs 22:6, NKJV).

As a kid, there was this saying that I would always hear parents use on their child. "Do as I say, not as I do," which is very hypocritical. For instance, I always find it odd how some parents would curse around their children and even curse at them, but as soon as their child uses that same kind of language, they're shocked and appalled. As parents, we have to be an example to our kids. Not only tell them what's right but show them what's right. We have to show our children what it looks like to surrender your life to Jesus Christ and live for God. For the most part, what a parent does speaks louder to their child than what they say.

✦

"My brethren, let not many of you become teachers, knowing that we shall receive a stricter judgment" (James 3:1, NKJV).

When God entrusts you with the care of His sheep and His Word, you are held to a different standard.

✦

When you aren't being led by God, you can be led to the wrong place at the wrong time. Let God lead you.

"Order my steps in thy word: and let not any iniquity have dominion over me" (Psalm 119:133, KJV).

✦

"Yet Michael the archangel, in contending with the devil, when he disputed about the body of Moses, dared not bring against him a reviling accusation, but said,

'The Lord rebuke you!'" (Jude 1:9, NKJV).

Why would the devil want the body of Moses after he died? It would seem that he tried to use his body as a vessel. The devil wanted to inhabit the body of Moses to lead the children of Israel away from God, knowing that they followed Moses because he was their leader. Which isn't too far-fetched since the devil will do this in the end times. Come in human form.

"The coming of the lawless one is according to the working of Satan, with all power, signs, and lying wonders" (2 Thessalonians 2:9, NKJV).

Mimicking God coming in the form of His Son, Jesus Christ.

"In the beginning was the Word, and the Word was with God, and the Word was God. [...] And the Word was made flesh, and dwelt among us, (and we beheld his glory, the glory as of the only begotten of the Father,) full of grace and truth" (John 1:1, 14, KJV).

In John 14:30 (NKJV), Jesus says, "For the ruler of this world is coming, and he has nothing in Me." There was nothing inside of Jesus that resembled the devil. The enemy wants his characteristics to be in us so that he can have more ground in our life to maneuver and lead us in the wrong direction.

That is why leaders need to ensure that they are being led by the Holy Spirit and not a demonic spirit. Leaders need to have Christlike character, not ungodly character. Being careful to guard themselves against anything the enemy tries to place in them.

CHAPTER 10

Made in the Wilderness

"Immediately the Spirit drove Him into the wilderness. And He was there in the wilderness forty days, tempted by Satan, and was with the wild beasts; and the angels ministered to Him" (Mark 1:12–13, NKJV).

WILDERNESS

Believers know about Jesus being in the desert, fasting for forty days, and being tempted by Satan. There is one small detail that is often overlooked. The verse says that "the Spirit drove Him into the wilderness." Jesus has been led by the Spirit of God and placed in the wilderness. By definition, a wilderness is described as a neglected or abandoned area, so in the wilderness, you can feel alone, but you have to trust in God's Word that says He will never leave you nor forsake you. The wilderness is also described as a place of disfavor. Life doesn't feel fair in the wilderness. It feels like the odds are stacked up against you, and every day has a disadvantage for you. You learn how to lean on God to get you through in the wilderness because only He can help you. God will help you because your help comes from the Lord. When you are in the wilderness, it's hard to see yourself getting out because you feel stuck. Isaiah 43:19 (KJV) says, "Behold, I will do a new thing; now it shall spring forth; shall ye not know it? I will even make a way in the wilderness, and rivers in the desert." God is saying, "What you thought was a dead-end, I'm going to turn into an outlet. A path that leads directly towards My promise and what I have prepared for you."

FORTY DAYS

The time that Jesus was in the wilderness was for forty days. That's a long time to be in those kinds of conditions, and many people naturally don't make it. They fall out and can't continue. Faith in God is fuel and energy for the believer to keep them going. You have to make sure that your faith isn't overcome by doubt and causes you to give up. Keep moving forward, keep trusting God, no matter how hard it gets.

FASTING

Jesus fasted while in the wilderness. He had no food, and some would say no water. He was in the wilderness, and He didn't have the everyday basic needs to survive. There was no abundance of resources; it was an extreme lack. Jesus, later on, goes on to say that men shall not live by bread alone, but by every word that proceeds from the mouth of God (Matthew 4:4). You may not have what you need, but if you have a Word from God, that's everything. That's what's going to make the difference. The Word of God will sustain you. The Word of God will protect you. The Word of God will guide you. The Word of God is the substance for your spirit.

Another thing that Jesus fasting in the wilderness is doing is preparing Him for ministry.

> Is this not the fast that I have chosen:
> To loose the bonds of wickedness,
> To undo the heavy burdens,
> To let the oppressed go free,
> And that you break every yoke?
>
> ISAIAH 58:6 (NKJV)

Jesus is being prepared to loose the bonds of wickedness, undo heavy burdens, set the oppressed free, and break yokes in people's lives. The wilderness is where we get equipped to minister to people, where we get anointed. In fact, how can you tell someone God can make a way out of no way if you don't know what it's like to feel like our life is going down the drain and God brings us out?

TEMPTED

Satan was also tempting Jesus in the wilderness. Another word for "tempted" is to be "tried." Jesus was being tried by Satan. The enemy wanted to see if he could entice Jesus away from God's purpose for His life. You know the devil is not threatened by us knowing the Word or believing in God. What you do with what you know about God is when the threat comes in. We cause problems for the enemy when we live by and stand on the Word of God. When we speak the Word over our lives and into certain situations commanding it to change. We have to speak the Word of God out of our mouths so it will penetrate the atmosphere and cause our surroundings to bend to God's will and change in our favor. The enemy tries us, and it's allowed because opposition makes us stronger. When pressure is applied, then you see what you can handle. It's in these conditions that God develops us and shows us what He's placed on the inside. It shows us that we can trust Him.

IF YOU ARE?

One thing the devil said to Jesus while He was in the wilderness is, "If thou be the Son of God, command that these stones be made bread" (Matthew 4:3, KJV).

The devil tries to get us to question who we are because he knows there's power in identity. The enemy will try and hit you with so much to the point where you question who God is and who you are in God. When you don't know who you are, it brings confusion, and the enemy can work and maneuver where there's confusion. When you are confused about who you are, you'll be confused about your purpose in life. So, it's important to know who God called you to be and your authority Christ. "Behold, I give you the authority to trample on serpents and scorpions, and over all the power of the enemy, and nothing shall by any means hurt you" (Luke 10:19, NKJV). The devil may come against you, but he is kept on a short leash when you are a child of God.

BEAST

There were wild beasts also in the wilderness with Jesus. He was surrounded by enemy forces. You ever look around, and it seems like everything is against you. Trouble is coming from every direction. You feel outnumbered, and you don't know how things are going to turn out. Know that God is for you and will help fight your battles.

"For the Lord your God is the one who goes with you to fight for you against your enemies to give you victory" (Deuteronomy 20:4, NIV).

ANGELS

Before Jesus exited the wilderness, angels ministered to Him. King David once said, "I will lift up my eyes to the hills—From whence comes my help? My help comes from the Lord, Who made heaven and earth" (Psalm 121:1–2, NKJV). God will send help from above. God will send someone who knows Him and has been in His presence to minister to you.

Lastly, you will not remain in the wilderness forever. You will come out because God will not abandon you. There are things that God needs to do in you that cannot be done outside of the wilderness. It's not to be looked at as something that's unfair because Jesus Himself went through the wilderness experience. In your walk with God, know that if He is leading you and you find yourself in the wilderness, He will lead you out. Just like how the Holy Spirit led Jesus to and through the wilderness, He will guide you through too. Amen.